ALEXANDER CAMPBELL

PREACHER OF REFORM AND
REFORMER OF PREACHING

ALEXANDER CAMPBELL

*Preacher of Reform and
Reformer of Preaching*

Alger Morton Fitch, Jr.

 SWEET PUBLISHING COMPANY
AUSTIN   TEXAS

Library of Congress Catalog Card Number: 70-113160
SBN 8344-0060-X

Acknowledgments

Appreciation is gratefully extended to **The Christian Standard**
for granting permission to include in chapter one portions of
the article "Recent Developments in the Study of Alexander
Campbell," which appeared in their May 13, 1965 issue; and
to the Disciples of Christ Historical Society, Nashville, Tenn.,
for supplying photographs of the Campbell manuscripts for
inclusion in this book.

Manufactured in the United States of America

CONTENTS

I NEW RESOURCES FOR CAMPBELL STUDY

The past decade has witnessed an increased interest on the part of a limited number of scholars in the church reformer Alexander Campbell (1788-1866). The growing attention to Campbell remains largely within the religious groups influenced by his leadership.

Since the Christian churches (Disciples of Christ) and the churches of Christ constitute the largest religious communion originating on American soil, it might have been expected that works dealing with American church history would give significant space to this preacher, debator, editor, educator, and statesman.

The facts have been otherwise. H. Shelton Smith, Robert T. Handy, and Lefferts A. Loetscher devote two lengthy volumes to *American Christianity, an Historical Interpretation with Representative Documents* (New York: Scribner, 1960). In the first, covering the period 1607-1820, Alexander Campbell shares a small paragraph with his father, Thomas. In the second, which goes beyond 1820 to the present, the name of Alexander Campbell can be found but once in the 634 pages. This sparse notice of the man Campbell by non-Disciples is typical.

An exception might be *The Sage of Bethany: a Pioneer in Broadcloth* (St. Louis: The Bethany Press, 1960) in which Roland Herbert Bainton of Yale University has contributed two chapters to the compiler, Perry Epler Gresham. Yet, even this study was requested and financed by the Bethany College which Alexander Campbell had founded in 1840. In 1956 Bainton had delivered the Oreon E. Scott lectures on "Alexander Campbell and Church Unity" at this school in West Virginia.

Many implements were used by Campbell in hewing out the message of Christian unity by a return to apostolic practice—a religious journal, a Christian college, a debate platform, a modern translation of the New Testament. A most effective instrument he used for the plea of "catholic" and primitive Christianity was that of preaching. Campbell's preaching left a lasting and deep impression upon even difficult places, trying conditions and rock-hard skeptics. He affirmed that "there is more proof in a spoken, than in a written gospel," for an oral delivery contains "all the warmth and power of the human voice" and the "additional testimony of the preacher himself."[1]

In our time there is an ascending interest in the person of Alexander Campbell, in the place of preaching and in the concept of church renewal. This book seeks to relate all three topics, viewing Alexander Campbell as a reformer of preaching and preacher of reform. (The "reform" he advocated was the renewal "of sinners, of Christians, and of religious institutions."[2])

Difficulties long have been recognized in recovering Campbell as a preacher. Mrs. Campbell, regretting that her husband "never desired or thought it important to have his discourses printed," claimed to know of only three in print: (1) the "Sermon on the Law" (2) the "Justification and Coronation of the Messiah" and (3) the "Riches of Christ."[3] Few sermons are extant and even of these we must ask: "Are they representative?" Except for the last sermon, which was written for D. S. Burnett's paper *The Christian Preach-*

er (1836), the others were written after delivery, and sometimes much later. Are these recalled accurately, since no notes were used in his extemporaneous style? Campbell's students allowed their records of his college lectures to be printed. Since his reaction to these in print was that such outlines proved to be "naked, meagre, and consequently, inadequate,"4 would he think better of W. K. Pendleton's attempt to print his father-in-law's New Year sermon of 1851 ("The Proper Use of Time")? That message would not be recovered from a transcript but only from recollection and a lifetime acquaintance with his style?5

The situation is not as hopeless as it sounds. Campbell wrote extensively for a lifetime and said much about preaching. He lectured, debated and gave addresses on a host of themes; and the relation between preparing and delivering a speech on a secular theme is suggestive regarding a sermon on a religious subject. Contemporaries in private correspondence and the public press tell of Campbell's preaching. He, himself, places in his periodicals full sermons by others which impressed him, as well as short messages by himself.6 Some of these he calls by the term "sermon"—i.e., "Sermons on Prayer—No. I," "Short Sermons for Business Men—No. 8," *etc.*7 Many articles in over forty years of editorial labor do not carry the word "sermon," but are certainly little different from what Campbell might teach to a Sunday morning church assembly. Besides, the biography of Campbell, as well as the periodicals by Campbell, give many sermon outlines he used with comments on their development. Campbell's book, *Familiar Lectures on the Pentateuch*, contains a section entitled "Extracts from President Campbell's Sermons."8

More encouraging now than even the references to Campbell's preaching by his contemporaries, or to Campbell's references to preaching in his various books and periodicals, are the newly found Campbell manuscripts that have been found in Australia.

Mrs. Decima Campbell Barclay, daughter of Alexander Campbell passed away in 1920. Her son, Julian, then left America for Australia with his daughter (Mrs. A. A. Andrews) and a trunk containing some of her great-grandfather's writings. These rare materials remained stored in the trunk at the farm in Algate some fourteen miles south of Adelaide. Here they fortunately escaped the destruction of a brush fire which three times started to burn the house, but each time was overcome.

When this forgotten trunk and its contents recently came to the attention of Mrs. Andrews, she gave them to her cousin, Mrs. E. V. Lawton of Hawthorne, because Mrs. Lawton alone of the family had remained in fellowship with the Australian Churches of Christ. I. J. Chivell, secretary of the South Australia Churches of Christ Evangelistic Union, Incorporated, and David G. Whyatt, their archivist, had the find microfilmed. During the South Australian State Conference held at the Adelaide Town Hall, Mr. E. V. Lawton, on September 8, 1964, presented the microfilm to the acting general secretary of the World Convention of Churches of Christ, Dr. Laurence V. Kirkpatrick of New York. On October 6, 1964, he in turn deposited the microfilm with the Disciples of Christ Historical Society at their annual banquet held during the Detroit assembly of the International Convention of Christian Churches (Disciples of Christ), The Historical Society's bi-monthly *Discipliana*, dated November, 1964, announced the immediate availability of microfilm copies. The original manuscripts were turned over to the Society at the World Convention in Puerto Rico in August of 1965.

Both Personal and Public

Claude E. Spencer calls this "the greatest find of primary materials since the Society was formed in 1941."[9] A more final verdict on historical value can be given only after the jury of scholars can investigate the new evidence. The condition of the manuscripts is good, allowing for the tendency of ink to fade and paper to discolor because of inadequate housing. Some pages are torn and others difficult to decipher. Among the variety of materials, we find some that was written with no thought of a future reader (such as sermonic notes intended to aid the preacher himself), and some that was prepared with exquisite penmanship for the eyes of others (such as a poem for professor, class, and friends in the University of Glasgow). The latter is often as difficult to read as the former, due to fading, plus the shading and artistic lettering attempted with a dip pen.

The historian now, for the first time, has at his disposal original materials reflecting the early thought of Alexander Campbell.

In long hand at Bethany, Campbell began listing receipts for moneys paid out from July 6, 1843, or recording the number and valuation of ewes, bucks, and lambs. This receipt book contains the note of a daughter dated December 9, 1899, which points to the first entry fifty-six years prior and gives the reasons for now making the book her notebook. Her mother, Selina Huntington Campbell, has placed in the same book such items as recipes, "Protection against moths," "how to tell when death sets in" [1873], grocery lists, and so forth.

A manuscript labeled "D," being written carefully and divided by chapters, indicates the author's awareness of possible readers. It is titled "Journal of a Voyage from Ireland Towards America," 1808. The eyewitness account, begun at Quiet Hill, Province of Ulster, gives details ranging from names of passengers to the lists of food and drink aboard.

Manuscripts E and F each contain Campbell's notes for thirteen sermons; and manuscript D and No. 332 each hold thirty-four sermons; in addition there are records regarding when, where and what was preached while Campbell was just out of his teen years.

ALEXANDER CAMPBELL

Disciplines of a Scholar

Like many a modern at the turn of a year, Campbell thought of resolutions and records. The beginning of a diary is among the materials found. Its first entry is January 1, 1809, and in fancy, shaded writing carries the poem "On the New Year." An 1810 resolution reveals his self-discipline through scheduling daily Bible study and memorization, plus the reading of Hebrew, Greek, Latin, poetry, philosophy, and composition.

Two itemizations should prove fruitful to those interested in the history of Christian thought and Campbell's place in that history. One is a list of books he had read "from his marriage" to his "going to live with Mrs. Brown March 25, 1811." This supplements another list of books he records as those taken with him on a trip and a further list of books he had earlier purchased. Present scholars, knowing the fruit of Campbell's mature thought during the years of editing and debating, may be assisted in tracing back the roots of that thought.

The other itemization referred to is that of the 106 sermons Campbell preached in the first year of his ministry (1811).

Having this enumeration of title or topic, text, date, and place we should be able to judge the development of his ideas and ideals, as well as to make a few needed corrections in dating. For example, Disciple historians had assumed that the famed "Sermon on the Law," which led to the severing of relations with the Baptists, was first preached on August 30, 1816. The new material lists this sermon as delivered earlier at the Brush Run church near Washington, Pennsylvania, on October 23, 1812.

His first public sermon preached at Buffalo, Major Temple, July 15, 1810, on Matthew 7:24-27 was repeated in Washington on September 9 of the same year. A study of his technique of sermon development with "introduction," "heads," "particulars," and "application," and of his practice of repeating the same message to different audiences, will be of interest to students of homiletics.

More important than the bare lists of title and text—to those interested in theology and history—will be the information in the newly-found skeleton sermons. Since most of the sermons were expositions of Scripture passages, Campbell's use and understanding of Scripture, his hermeneutical principles, and his later continuance or change in thinking can be discovered. Someone will want to analyze his early message "Why Not Join a Party?" in the light of his place in the plea for Christian unity. Another may care to consider "On the Name Christian" with Barton Warren Stone's preference for that name over Campbell's contention for "disciple of Christ." Still another may desire to compare "Presbyterian" Campbell's thought on ecclesiology in the sermon "Church Government," delivered to the Washington Association, to that in a different message titled "Paul's Qualifications for Bishops."

In the face of public interest in Campbell's doctrine of baptism, sermon outlines on John 3:3 or the "New Covenant" will gain attention. Those believing Campbell to hold a teaching of "water salvation" or "baptismal regeneration" will ponder subdivision two of an old message on Genesis 3:7-10 which, in answer to the question, "Who is so foolish as to plait fig leaves to cover their nakedness?" replies: "Such as trust to their baptism."

A glance at Campbell's choice of Bible passages shows preference for New Testament texts. The few sermons from the Old Testament either show the New Testament church in the typology of the ancient tabernacle or temple, pointing up the ancient prophecies that found their fulfillment in Christ, or they make some stress on the new covenant's supersedence over the old. And exception to this limited use of the Old Testament is the consistent use of the book of Psalms, the hymnbook of ancient Israel, and the hymnal used in the manse of Thomas and Alexander Campbell, which was the Scotch Psalter of Sir Francis Rous.

A Taste for Poetry

At this point we can suggest the light that the new materials may throw on Campbell in the area of poetry and hymnody. It has been known that he wrote five hymns and one or two poems, and edited a hymnal. In "Extracts and Original Essays by Alexander Campbell in Glasgow, 1809," he states that the poems therein were written "at various opportunities for self improvement" and to "correct my [his] taste."

In a work entitled "Poems" he tells the occasion of each and then records the ode written at that time. There are eleven in all and they are not in chronological order, although all were written in 1809-1810. Some are lengthy. Most are neatly copied but others have words and lines marked out. The poems are inspired by a class assignment, a tragedy, a natural wonder, etc. They reflect a student of the classics trying his hand at the art.

"Advantages and Disadvantages of Holy-days" and "Attempt to Translate Ovid's Account of the Golden Age" suggest the type of subject matter dealt with and show it not to be the Scriptures which later inspired his hymns.

The new materials, however, do contain also the "versification of Luke 1:46-55" and "versification of Luke 1:68-79," reminiscent of the Psalter. Campbell had also copied four songs, the last two, at least, from the hymnal of the followers of the Scotch Independent John Glas. In a big scrawl getting larger by the verse, as if copied in a hurry, are three verses of "Hymn First," "Come Let Us Join in Songs of Praise"; the six stanzas of "How Are Thy Servants

Blessed, O Lord"; the four verses of "Hymn 4," "Praise Ye Jehovah's Love and Grace"; and "Song 12," "God's Mercies We Will Ever Sing."

These new facts may suggest sources, standards, and style effecting the hymnal *Psalms, Hymns and Spiritual Songs* which he edited from 1828 until his death.

The "Essays" on themes always favorite to Campbell will add to our concept of his ideas on "Democracy," "Education," "Ordination," and the like. The letter to a Mrs. Smith on "Justification" will help the theologian understand Campbell's soteriology. The "Lectures on Greek *MI* Verbs" dealing with syntax, parsing, and poor translation will interest others.

The "Rules on Feeding Cattle" will excite fewer Disciples of Christ. But, many students of the American church will agree that as past scholarly works on Alexander Campbell have related him and his thought to the whole of Christian history, the new manuscript discovery will answer some questions and raise others for scholars to write about during the coming years.

The Scope of the Present Work

Of major concern for this book, however, are Campbell's sermonic materials. In the unity movement he championed, Campbell stressed the vital place of preaching in the life of the church. The above-mentioned newly-discovered materials make possible a fresh look at and a more comprehensive study of Campbell's sermonic views. The last work in the area of Campbell's preaching concept was made by Granville T. Walker in 1954.[10]

Through a re-examination of old sources and a critical study of new ones, we propose to re-evaluate Campbell's preaching and rediscover those relevant and lasting insights which bring renewal to Christ's church in any age. The purpose of this book is to demonstrate that Alexander Campbell not only proved to be an efficient preacher of reform, he presented to the world a reform for preaching.

Using illustrations from Campbell's own preaching experiences, Part One will analyze Campbell's proposed reforms in preaching. After a consideration of the status of preaching at his time, in contrast to the ideal for preaching in apostolic times, the further chapters of Part One will look to Campbell's understanding regarding apostolic concepts of preaching, preachers, audiences, and sermons. Part two will view Campbell's life as a preacher. In five chapters, we will review his background, ministry, sermons, and influence.

PART ONE

ALEXANDER CAMPBELL: REFORMER OF PREACHING

II NEEDS AND NORMS
The Situation

Preachers not only preach, they hear preaching. Having in their own minds a concept of what constitutes a good sermon, they are generally more critical than others in the church regarding what they hear from the pulpit. Alexander Campbell was no exception. He had unwavering convictions as to what the sermon should be, and he had uninhibited reactions to what passed for preaching in his time.

On the one hand he responded negatively to the revivalistic sermons heard on the American frontier. Equally so, he chilled under the cold theologies of the past that were served to hungering sheep by shepherds more loyal to the party line than to the apostolic and prophetic word.

The former—preachers of the Great Revival—fired up the feelings of their hearers, if they did not build up their Biblical knowledge. Facts and evidence could firm up confidence. Emotional appeals could only stir up tears or ejaculations. In the South, especially among the Baptists with whom Campbell early associated, many considered emotional excitement as "the evidence, if not the very essence of religion."[1] Campbell recalled:

> I have seen other preachers who can strike fire no other way than by the friction of their hands, and an occasional clap, resembling a peal of distant thunder. In this holy paroxysm of clapping, rubbing, sneezing, and roaring, the mind is fairly on the way, and the tongue

in full gallup, which like a race horse, runs the swifter the less weight it carries . . . They can neither speak to God nor man in the pulpit to purpose, as they think, unless when, like the boiler of a steam boat, they are almost ready to burst.[2]

On one occasion in New York Campbell heard the man who converted Charles Grandison Finney (1792-1875). He described Samuel Dickinson Burchard (1812-1891) as

impassioned in his oratory, illogical in much of his reasoning, and extremely hazardous in his quotations and applications of scripture—vehement, boisterous, and declamatory, he compels his audience to be prayed for, and will have them on the penitential benches whether or not. Like a tornado in passing through the country, he upturns everything that can be moved.[3]

The case for Christianity in all its reasonableness could be addressed to the mind of man with no need for convulsions or contortions, swoonings or trances. The necessity of the hour was a rational examination of divinely-given evidence and not revivalism's emotional orgies. Campbell's unbending resistance to the "warm preaching," "uninspired harangues," and "enthusiasm" of the revivals caused charges to be brought against him as a denier of the Holy Spirit and "experimental religion." This he disavowed[4] and argued that being filled with the Spirit and led by the Spirit were not the equivalent of being filled with ignorance regarding Scripture and led astray by our feelings. He wrote:

Ignorance is often the mother of enthusiasm or superstition, either of which is, with many, equivalent to devotion. Many of those unlettered divines who are supposed to speak entirely from the Spirit, for everyone knows it is not from a fund of knowledge or from literary attainments which they possess, are indeed as evidently without the grace of God as his holiness the pope or his grace the duke of York. They speak from the spirit, but it is from the spirit of enthusiasm. Enthusiasm is frequently accompanied with a remarkable volubility of speech and pathos of expression. There are none more eloquent nor more ungrammatical than the enthusiastic. Indeed, some writers on eloquence of the highest order say that this kind of eloquence is the creature of enthusiastic ardore. Thousands of ignorant unlettered men, not fettered by the rules of grammar, not circumscribed by the restraints of reason, nor controlled by the dictates of common sense, nor limited by the written word of God, are nevertheless both fluent, and, though incorrect, eloquent speakers they are elevated by enthusiasm and like the meteors of the night, shine with more resplendence than the real stars.[5]

Observation showed that summer would be followed by winter and that the revival heat, based on emotional fever rather than on reason and revelation, would be turned into coldness. There was evidence of no root in those who were converted to either their own feelings or to a phantom rather than to Christ through understanding.[6]

Where behind one sacred desk might stand a revivalist relating his own subjective experiences by one anecdote after another; in a different pulpit the other extreme might be represented by a denominationalist defending his own sect's definitions by one proof-text after another.

Metaphysics and theology were to Campbell inadequate substitutes for the gospel of Christ. Treating the Bible as a volume of proof texts to be martialed to the support of church tenets or creedal affirmations, was mistreating the Scripture. If the Bible was to reprove, rebuke, correct and instruct the church, the church would need to listen to the written word in its fulness and not to select only what appeared to say "amen" to the preacher's own statement of faith.

Listening with other auditors to a Presbyterian clergyman in Iowa, Campbell lamented over the discourse: "If true as mathematics, it was as cold as zero, and as inoperative as fluxions, or as the *differential* and *integral* Calculus. I know not whether my sympathies for the preacher or for the hearers predominated. But certainly I sympathized with both."[7]

The popular method of preaching from a text received the blame for lay ignorance of the Scripture and clerical proclamation of party doctrine. The people were bewildered rather than enlightened by the "modern moral philosophers and Christian Doctors" who were little more than "retailers of scraps."[8] Instead of discussing a subject in the light of the whole Bible, they took a text—often a verse or a portion of a verse—sometimes but three words. On such a limited base the preaching of two or three hours followed with no reference to the context or to the biblical author's purpose.

To use a text for a "motto,"[9] and then to proceed by preaching the opinions of a council or the subjective experiences of one's own life, was to call on the congregation to suffer their faith to rest not in the wisdom of God but in the wisdom of men.[10] By divorcing text from context and following worn-out hermeneutical principles, "textuaries" made passages of Scripture teach anything the pulpiteer desired. Spiritualizing verses and indulging in mystical flights of the imagination did not inform the hearers what the Bible said, but let them join in following the futile meanderings of a dark and foolish mind. Such a preacher was not preaching Christ but himself. Saying what one pleased, and placing it all to the account of a detached sentence previously read, was neither speaking where the Scriptures were speaking nor being silent where they were silent.

The meaning of "textuary" or "textual preaching" must be learned from Campbell's understanding of the word "text." He stated:

> I do not know whether we ought to agree with those lexicographers who make the Roman *textus* a term equi-

valent to the Grecian *ploke*, a weaving. Some may justi-
fy this etymological interpretation, because, they may
suppose, that there is an analogy between the making of
a web from thread, and the weaving of a sermon from a
few detached words, called a *text*. I would rather derive
the term *text* directly from the Greek verb *texto*, to be-
get or bring forth, from which *texos* or *textus* might be
ingeniously formed, and this might be translated an egg,
or something pregnant with life, which by the laws of
nature might become a living animal, as a text by the
laws of sermonizing easily becomes a full grown sermon.[11]

Campbell often directed his co-workers' attention to the
ignorance of the Bible that stemmed from the practice of
"text-preaching."

He wrote in 1824:

But you who occupy the pulpit, are the very persons
who are to blame for the incapacity. This useless and
senseless way of talking which you call preaching, into
which the old pagans led you, is the very way to make
the people ignorant, to confound, perplex, and stupify
them. This everlasting sermonizing, what good is it?
It resembles nothing that is rational in all the compass
of thought. A B professes to teach arithmetic; he gets
a class of forty boys from 12 to 15 years old, we shall
say. He tells them to meet once-a-week and he will give
them a lecture or a sermon on some important point
in this useful science. The first day he lectures on the
cube root for an hour. They sit bookless and thought-
less, heedless, and, perhaps often drowsy, while he
harangues them. He blesses them and sends them home,
to return a week hence. They meet. His text is arith-
metical progression. He preaches an hour; dismisses as
usual. The third day of the meeting up comes vulgar
fractions; the fourth, rule of three, the fifth, addition;
the sixth, notation; the seventh, cube root again, &c.
&c. (*sic*). Now in this way, I hesitate not to say, he

might proceed seven years and not finish one accountant. Whoever thought that a science or an art could be taught this way! And yet this is the only way, I may say, universally adopted of teaching the Christian religion. And so it is that many men have sat under the sound gospel (as they call it) for forty years that cannot expound one chapter in the whole New Testament. And yet these same Christians would think it just to prosecute by civil law that teacher who would keep their sons four or five years at English grammar or arithmetic, who receive their money, and yet not one of their sons able to expound one rule in syntax or arithmetic.[12]

In 1853 he was found still pressing the same point and following the same illustration.

Not one Rabbi in one thousand, either intends or expects his church ever to graduate in Christian learning, or in the knowledge of the Christian Scriptures. "Ever learning, but never able to arrive at the knowledge" of the Christian text-book, seems to be the doom and destiny of every community that lives and dies under the textuary theologues of the 19th century. The *five points*, or the thirty-nine articles, may be taught and learned in Sunday schools or churches; but what church in any community understands Paul to the Romans, or Paul to the Hebrews?—! If Methuselah were to live again his nine hundred, sixty and nine years, and to spend them all in one community, under the textuary system of the best Protestant sectary amongst us, listening to him as our auditors do in Protestant Churches, could he say, "I understand the volume?!"[13]

In setting forth principles and objects for the healing of divisions among Christians, the Reformer called for a restoration of the terms of the Bible, the treatment of the Bible as a book of history, the use of the Bible in the place of creeds, and fourthly—but, in our point of inquiry, first—"The reading and expounding of the sacred scriptures in public assemblies instead of text preaching, sermonizing, and philosophizing . . . "This scheme has filled the pulpit with a race of pigmies in the Bible as diminutive as ever lived."[13]

Was there an alternative to bare emotionalism on the one hand and on the other to the dignified dullness of a "dry, formal, philosophical, and speculative sermonizing, falsely called preaching the gospel?"[15] Instead of the textuary system that allowed for both unsatisfactory types of preaching, Campbell proposed a return to the Bible for the manner as well as the matter of proclamation.[16] Other books besides the Bible influenced Campbell, but not as consciously. Other biblical books besides Luke's Acts of the Apostles were guides to his preaching, yet not as predominantly.

Robert Richardson, for example, noted a memorandum of 1809 where young Campbell had copied from Dr. Beattie's *Ethics* six rhetorical principles "necessary to attain excellence in the composing and pronouncing of sermons." Campbell's biographer stated that he inserted these rules because his subject seemed "to have been impressed by their justness, and to have modeled himself by them in his future course as a preacher."[17] This may have been true of Campbell unconsciously. Yet, on later occasions, Campbell was the first to remind the people that he underwent many unexpected reformations when he set out to make the Bible alone his standard. In recalling an early sermon he preached (June, 1811), he remarked: "We were all Pedobaptists, and in our mode of preaching and teaching more textuary and formal than we have since learned is either scriptural or advantageous to speaker or hearer."[18]

If Protestants generally looked to Augustine or the schoolmen for homiletical style, those wishing to be known as simply disciples of Christ were to look beyond these to Old and New Testament models. Deuteronomy was a series of sermons by Moses to the Jews and exemplified the simple but full relating of God's doings and man's actions during the wilderness experience of forty years, plus the arguments, exhortations and applications drawn from these facts. Ezra and Nehemiah's example of speaking to a people in captivity was instructive to reformers leading people out of a later "Babylonian" captivity.[19] Christ, certainly, was a master preacher; and his method of teaching was a major concern of those who would teach others. That Jesus was not a theoretical but a practical preacher was the burden of Campbell's sermon on the Sermon on the Mount.[20] Richardson reflected Campbell's insight when he wrote of Christ's sermon:

. . . we perceive that he did not, like modern theologians, commence his religious teachings by laying down definitions and prescribing articles of faith. He does not begin by saying that God is a being "without body or parts," neither does he deliver propositions concerning "original sin," or "free-will," or set himself to regulate "Rites, Ceremonies and Sacraments." On the contrary, he begins by pronouncing a blessing upon the "poor in spirit;" upon the "mourner," and upon the "meek," upon those who "hunger and thirst" for righteousness; upon the "merciful;" the "pure in heart;" the "peacemakers," and the "persecuted." He instructs his disciples to "let their light so shine before men that they may see their *good works* and glorify their Father in heaven." He teaches them *to act* like children of God, in loving their enemies, doing good to those that hated them, and in praying for their persecutors. He delivers throughout rules of life and conduct;—heart-teachings; heart-exhortations; soul-saving principles of action . . . Christs "sayings" then, had respect to things that were *to be done*, and not to matters of opinion and questions of theology.[21]

Beyond the inspired preaching *by* Christ there was the inspired preaching *about* Christ recorded in Acts. The apostolic model of proclaiming Jesus was God's divinely authorized example of how to preach. In his periodical and for the reader's imitation Campbell analyzed the seven speeches found in the Book of Acts. He lectured on this theme from time to time[22] and his apology for the call to return to preaching as "in the beginning" was that the "same mint" was essential to the "same coin." He added:

We do this for the sake of directing the attention of our fellow-laborers to the philosophy of the Bible, and to the folly of attempting the conversion of sinners by a display of controversial, speculative, and dogmatic theology. The primitive preachers announced the wonderful works and designs of Heaven in sending the Messiah into the world, from which they deduced motives rationally and morally adapted to effect the change of disposition, state, and character which the gospel proposes as prerequisite to a glorious immortality.[23]

Alexander Campbell, upon looking about at the preaching in his time, saw much to be desired. The revivalists were preaching their opinions and their experiences. The traditionalists were proclaiming their creeds and their theologies. He asked if preaching Christianity was the same as preaching Christ? If proclaiming the Holy Spirit in every paragraph was what the New Testament meant by preaching Jesus? If heralding the Law was the same as announcing the Gospel? If a preacher's constant assertion that he was a gospel preacher made him one?

Seeing a need Campbell sought a norm. It was not to be found in his immediate past, for the practice of the Anti-Burger Seceder Presbyterian clergy was like that found elsewhere. By taking a text and immediately departing into a world of thought never imagined by the Paul or the David who penned the words God's church was kept ignorant of his will. The Bible was claimed to be sufficient to make the man of God sufficient. Believing this, Campbell called for all teachers and preachers under his influence to restudy the ancient Scriptures for a sure answer to the questions "What should we preach?" "How should we preach?" "Who ought to preach?" and "When and where and why?"

The need was urgent. The norm was available. "To the law and to the testimony."

III TERMS AND TASKS
Preaching

Webster's Dictionary states that to preach is "to discourse publicly on a religious subject, or from a text of scripture; to deliver a sermon." It also states that to baptize is "to dip or immerse in water or to pour or sprinkle water upon, as a religious rite or ceremony." Neither definition could satisfy the Reformer who had determined to give biblical meanings to biblical terms.[1] What a word had come to mean through common usage was one thing. What Christ or his apostles had in mind when they used some term might be entirely different.

A discourse was not preaching just because it was delivered by a minister, spoken from a pulpit, or appended to a text. In his customary way of seeking accuracy in terminology, Campbell carefully distinguished between present and past usages as well as distinctions in the various scriptural words. He was confident that there was no inspired writer who made "a distinction without a difference."[2]

In an address before the Kentucky Convention of 1853, on "Church Edification" Campbell began:

Preaching the gospel and teaching the converts, are as distinct and distinguishable employments as enlisting an army and training it, or as creating a school and teaching it. Unhappily for the church and for the world, this distinction, if at all conceded as legitimate, is obliterated or annulled in almost all Protestant Christendom. The public heralds of Christianity, acting as missionaries or evangelists, and the elders or pastors of Christian churches, are indiscriminately denominated *preachers*, or minister; and whether addressing the church or the world, they are alike *preaching*, or ministering something which they call *the gospel*.[3]

An exploration of the New Testament established the fact that "preaching" and "teaching" were two works and in the apostolic church never were confused. The Pastoral Epistles instructed an evangelist to *"preach* the word;"* while they called for bishops "apt to *teach"* and able to convict gainsayers by "sound *teaching."* The apostles were commissioned to go into the world and *"preach* the gospel;"* but were instructed that after the baptism of the converts, they were to *"teach* them to observe" all that Christ had commanded. The historian Luke recorded that the early disciples ceased not "to *teach* and to *preach* Jesus Christ." Paul, who was ordained a *preacher* and a *teacher* of the truth among the Gentiles, declared again to the Corinthian converts what he had initially "preached" and already they had received.

If reading, writing and speaking were different activities; so were preaching, teaching and exhorting.[4] If preaching and baptizing were not the same act, even if performed by the same person; so neither were preaching and teaching. In *The Living Oracles*, the modern version of the New Testament published by Campbell, *kerygma* and the *didache* were rendered "proclamation" and "teaching."

> *Keerux*, the *preacher*, *keerussoo*, I *preach* and *Kerrugma* the speech, or the *preaching*—and also *euanggelistees* [*sic*] the evangelist, *euaggelion*, the gospel and *euaggelizoo*, I preach the gospel, frequently occur in the Greek Christian Scriptures—and are of nearly equal circulation; from *didaskoo*, I teach, *didaskalia* and *didachee* a doctrine, and *didaskalos* a teacher. No two such families of words of so many branches, and of so large a cur-

rency are more distinguishable or more frequently distinguished in the whole nomenclature of the Christian Scriptures.[5]

Preachers, in the biblical limitations of the word, were to solicit pupils for the school of Christ where teachers then would instruct them. Let preachers conquer men for Christ and let elders maintain the conquest. Let preachers obtain, and then let elders sustain the family of God. One announces salvation through Christ. The other develops the duties incumbent upon those who have placed themselves under Christ's guidance. To the world the gospel is preached. To the initiated (the church) the gospel is expounded.

Paul may have *declared* the gospel facts to the Corinthian church; but to the world outside the church he preached them.[6] News is reported, proclaimed, preached. No one teaches news or exhorts news.[7] Conversion is the end result of preaching; while progress and perfection are the goal of teaching. Simply put: "to make the fact known is to *preach*, and to explain the meaning of that fact is to *teach*."[8] These words were in Campbell's ears and mind as different in sense as in sound.[9]

Such a definitive look at preaching put real limitations on the preacher's subject matter. Preaching was for sinners and teaching for saints. If a preacher was a herald or proclaimer of news, he dealt in facts and events. As a patient needed medicine to cure his disease and not a lecture on the nature of his disease, or an analysis of the remedy, so the world needed the gospel more than a discourse about it.

The preacher announced or narrated the wonderful works of God in Christ. He was to state, illustrate and prove the great gospel facts, but he was not to proclaim a theory, a speculation or a philosophy. He was not to indoctrinate as if that would or could produce faith. He was not to preach Christianity but Christ. He could not even preach morality.

Such a topic is teachable but not preachable.[10]

No man, no philologist, can *preach doctrines*; but any one conversant with doctrines may *teach* them. We *proclaim*, we preach, we announce facts and events, and such are the materials of the gospel. It is no theory, no philosophy, no doctrine, no speculation, no abstraction, no logical deduction, but a series of the most animating, soul-stirring, soul-cheering, soul-exhilarating facts, events, precepts, promises, consolations, joys, beatitudes—"an exceeding and eternal weight of glory," honor and blessedness! Such is the blissful gospel, and the blissful work of proclaiming it to Jew or gentile, barbarian, Scythian, bond or free.[11]

The teacher of Christians was limited, likewise, by the Scripture. The apostles did not attempt to convert men by teaching but by preaching. Neither did they try to perfect the disciples by preaching. The "apostles' teaching" had to do not with tenets to be believed but with precepts to be obeyed. Baptized believers were to be taught to observe what was commanded by Christ. Jesus' teaching was not theoretical but practical; and it was intended, not to impart orthodox views, but to produce moral and spiritual lives.[12] An error crying out for reform was the supposition that the Christian faith was *doctrinal*, consisting of tenets; when it was *personal*, having to do with trust in Christ.

A second place where the church had gone awry was in imagining that its teachers were to make men *think* right; when their divinely given task was to teach them to *do* right. In church history recurred the sad record of some man who, though living the life of a Christian, was being debarred from Christian fellowship because he was Arminian, Calvinistic, or unorthodox according to the definitions of some school.

The failure of the nineteenth-century church to see this first century division between teaching and preaching led to the confusion of converting the church into the world and the world into the church. Pedobaptists had put the world into the church, according to Campbell, through infant baptism. Thus, they had always to preach the gospel to their church members in order to convert them, as if they were yet in the world. And, judging from the pulpit expositions, Baptists were more frequently found preaching conversion to their hearers than building them up in their faith.[13]

C. H. Dodd in his book, *The Apostolic Preaching*, with its analysis of the *kerygma* found in the sermons of Acts, plus modern form-criticism's recognition of the gospels as expanded *kerygma*, recognize the same distinction of *kerygma* and *didache*, preaching and teaching.

That this distinction is not so new is evident from a quotation in the *Millennial Harbinger* of June, 1846. An author who signed his name by the simple initial "N." quoted the Dr. Campbell upon whose translation work Alexander Campbell had relied for his modern version of the New Testament.

No moral instructions, or doctrinal explanations, given either by our Lord or his Apostles, are ever either in the Gospels or the Acts, denominated preaching . . . (*kerusso*) always implied public notice of some event, either accomplished or about to be accomplished, often accompanied by a warning to do, or forbear something, but it never denoted either a comment on, or an explanation of any subject.[14]

A distinction of work suggests a division of labor among the workers. No reader of the *Christian Baptist* was long in discovering that the return to the "ancient order of things" could begin only when the "kingdom of the clergy" was replaced by the more humble New Testament offices of evangelist, bishop and deacon.[15]

"Let us have no clergy at all, learned or unlearned," was Campbell's plea.[16] The clergy had usurped the rights and privileges of all believers. The clergy might be a creation patterned after all other religions; but it was not known to that religion initiated by Christ. However, all the laity—all the people of God—were to minister; and Christ had given certain members of his body revealing, preaching and teaching functions that were to prepare his other ministers to do their work more effectively.

When attacking the hireling clergy for their pretence of having priestly prerogatives or a sacerdotal ministry; he warned against a possible misunderstanding: "*Nota Bene.— In our remarks upon the Christian Clergy, we never include the Elders or Deacons of a Christian Assembly or those in the New Testament called Overseers and Servants of the Christian Church. These we consider as very different characters.*"[17]

Campbell set as his goal the overthrow of this class that he considered as a whole to be proud and self-seeking. He attacked their titles, party loyalty, clerical garb and sanctimonious speech.

In place of the seminary-trained, religious professional over the churches, he sought to reestablish the shepherding ministry of elders within the churches. As the ministry of Christ in the flesh was not to be repeated in every age, so the special ministry of the apostles that Jesus had selected possessed a "once for all" character. No present-day human could qualify as a witness of Christ's resurrection, pretend to apostolic powers, or claim such a direct call from heaven.

The apostles and prophets were officers extraordinary, necessary to the setting up of the Christian institution.[18] Once established, it only required an ordinary administration of affairs. Moses was endowed with miracle-power as the Jewish dispensation began. The "signs of an apostle" accompanied the establishment of the new Israel as well. Moses still spoke in the synagogues when his writings were read, and the apostles still ruled in the churches through the New Testament, the record of their preaching and teaching.

Whereas an apostle of Christ was one of the few disciples necessary to reveal and confirm the gospel story, an evangelist for Christ was one of the many disciples in every age and place necessary to make the apostolic witness known. The preacher, or evangelist, was a foreign minister of the church in contrast to the bishops who were domestic ministers. The latter were for building up the church at home and the former for founding new communities throughout the land.

Evangelists were called missionaries because this word suggested that they were sent and sustained by the church. The term evangelist derived from the nature of their work.[19] These gospel proclaimers might be sent by a particular congregation or by the whole church of a district[20] as Walter Scott had worked as an evangelist for the Mahoning Baptist Association.[21]

The work of an evangelist was to convert sinners, plant churches and assist in setting things in order. Such a work would be needed until the world and the church became coextensive. Then such a person would "not be necessary, any more than a standing army in time of peace."[22]

While in a lesser sense all were preachers, including the Psalmist's "heavens" that declared the glory of God.[23], there needed to be certain men especially set apart and devoted to this work. Each Christian in his private sphere was to publish the glad tidings. Still, the churches must send out public heralds who were to become wholly engrossed in the single work of reconciling men to God. Campbell wrote, "One business at a time is enough for the powers of any one man."[24] In *The Christian System* he wrote:

But we shall be asked, "Is not preaching, and baptizing, and even teaching, the common privilege of all disciples, as they have opportunity?" And we also ask in answer, "Is it not the privilege of all fathers to teach their own children and to preside over their own families?" But who will thence infer, that all fathers are teachers and presidents, does not more shock common sense, than he who infers that all disciples, as such, are evangelists, pastors, and teachers, because we concede that in certain cases it is the privilege of all the citizens of Christ's kingdom to preach, baptize, and teach. Every citizen of Christ's kingdom has, in virtue of his citizenship, equal rights, privileges, and immunities. So has every citizen of the United States. Yet all citizens are not legislators, magistrates, judges, governors, *etc.* Before any community, civil or religious, is organized, every man has equal rights to do what seemeth good in his own eyes. But when organized, and persons appointed to office, then whatever rights, duties, privileges are conferred on particular persons, can not of right belong to those who have transferred them; any more than a person can not both give and keep the same thing.[25]

These evangelists, though created by the church, did not serve it directly but were sent out into the world. They to whom a preacher spoke were not *his* people, "nor was he their preacher!"[26] The relationship, however, of pastors and people, shepherds and sheep, was quite otherwise. A pastor or teacher had a particular charge over which the brethren and the Holy Spirit had constituted him an overseer. Whereas the evangelists or preachers were for "marking the sheep and putting them into the green pastures," the elders were "for taking care of the sheep."[27] No overseer's tenure was perpetual or his authority universal.[28]

Each congregation was for its well-being to have a plurality of bishops. Every church in a city, and in most country places, was to strive to have at least one person wholly devoted to the pastoral office. Campbell observed: "whatever is every one's business, is no one's special duty."[29]

No man could be a pastor who had no specific pasture to tend. There had to be sheep before there could be a shepherd. There had to be the work to be done, before there could be a workman. Campbell penned: "A BISHOP without a charge or cure, is like a husband without a wife . . . a president without a people, a teacher without pupils . . . an eye without a head, a tongue without a mouth, a hand without a body."[30]

It was common among the Baptists, as among the Methodists of the time, to have circuit riders. Campbell could see circuit-riding preachers but not circulating pastors, even when the movement from church to church was limited to a few congregations. To catch his reasoning we lift out his own words prompted by a correspondence from Thomas Bullock of Kentucky:

As respects the four churches and one pastor, or the monthly rotation, or the "horsemill plan," as some call it; that is, in plain Scotch, one preacher coming once a month to preach to one church, in a regular round, as many times as there are months in a year—just as a blind horse, when he has gone once round, begins a second tour in the same track . . . Let every particular congregation elect one or more bishops who had never been spoiled by the preaching plan, and loose all the cords which bind these present preachers to four congregations, and let them go in circuits in rotation as often and as extensively as they could, and preach and teach; but let the congregations meet every Lord's day with their own bishops, and attend upon the ancient order of things; and when any of these circuit preachers made them a visit, let them exercise all the gifts they had for the edification of the brotherhood and the conversion of all around; but by no means to interfere with the stated worship of the day.[31]

Robert Richardson observed that Barton W. Stone, with whom Campbell was associated, was engaged mainly in

37

preaching while Campbell worked primarily at teaching.[32] Campbell had been a teacher in his father's school at Rice Hill in Ireland before he was ordained a preacher. His later work as an editor prohibited him from doing the work of an evangelist. Even when making extensive tours he set out, not so much to preach the ancient gospel for the purpose of converting sinners to God, as to disseminate the general principles of reform amongst the Christians.[33] Nevertheless, he held in his mind a clear concept of what he would do if he ever set out to preach and of what he would do when he was called upon to teach.

In 1822, under the pen name "Evangelicus," Campbell laid out the type of preaching exemplified in Acts that he would follow upon an invitation to that work.[34] In his many addresses on "Christian Edification" he pleaded for a regular assembly of the school of Christ:

The church members must punctually attend. They must not forsake or neglect the assembling of themselves together on the first day of the week.

They should carry with them, or have in their pews, the Holy Bible, and attend to all the readings, teachings, and exhortations of the eldership, book in hand.

The historical books, or the epistles written to the churches, should be taken up in order by the elder who officiates, who, of course, is apt to teach, and qualified to instruct the congregation.

The lesson for the day should be known before, and studied through the week. Several chapters may sometimes constitute but one lesson. A part of a chapter, or parable, a single paragraph may furnish an adequate theme for one meeting. These portions in regular sequence, read in the closet, or in the family, should always be preparatory studies, with reference to public meetings, for edification.

A lecture of half an hour, more or less, should be prepared by the President of the day. A brief exhortation is always opportune.[35]

Campbell longed for the day when persons would be "taught the Christian religion as good scholars are taught the sciences!"[36] Such a time would not appear unless the church could see its need and seek to return to the biblical norm of preaching and teaching. The first step back would be to find the scriptural meaning of the terms used and a biblical view of the tasks required. If anyone objected that he was quibbling about words, he had a reply:

To many it seems but of little consequence to be tenacious of the name. Why not then call all the leaders priests? Why not call them astrologers, soothsayers, or oneirocritics, if the name be indifferent? Because, says one, those names are used to denote quite different characters. For the same reason, therefore, let the names which the apostles adopted be used in their own acceptation, and let those things, persons, and offices which the apostles said nothing about, be named or styled as the inventers please; but call not bitter sweet, nor sweet bitter. Let us not call the messenger of a congregation, an elder. Let us not call a bishop, a divine; nor a deacon, a ruling elder. In a word, let us give to divine institutions divine names, and to human institutions human names.[37]

IV CALL AND CHARACTER
The Preacher

"Woe is me if I preach not the Gospel," wrote Paul. "Woe is me," thought many others, "if I would dare to preach at all, when God has not laid his hand upon me and especially called me to stand behind the sacred desk and to be his spokesman." What was Campbell's thinking regarding the call to preach or teach? To whom was the right and duty given? What character must a preacher possess?

Although Campbell was a preacher's son and probably had as many, or more, opportunities than others to assist in public worship, there is no trace of any attempt on his part to help conduct a public worship service until he was twenty-two years of age. Was this hesitency because of his feeling about the high qualifications demanded of a minister? This appears as a possibility, if we consider the journal he kept when a student at the University of Glasgow. In this book were copied seven rules for a preacher.[1] The first four of these were regarding essentials for ministerial character and training. Campbell had been influenced by the Haldanes who allowed for a lay ministry; but had he been freed completely from the common idea of a special, divine call?

Once having determined to apply the New Testament as norm to all religious questions, Campbell did just that in relation to the preachers themselves. His conclusion was that no clergyman of his day, nor of any day since the last apostle died, could make claim to a special divine call to preach. To claim a direct, divine call to preach was to place an audience under a divine call to listen to the public instructor. God would neither send a liar, nor one unacquainted with his will, nor one unaccomplished for the task. If the Holy Spirit sent the speaker, it would be criminal to despise his instructions. When apostles made such claims, they expected the recipients to accept the message as infallible. Were modern clergymen successors of the apostles as ambassadors of Christ?

When the editor of the *Christian Baptist* set out to deny clerics the right to such a claim, he referred to "Rev. Gideon Blackburn, D. D. Pastor of the Church in Louisville, Kentucky" and jibed:

> When therefore, the Holy Spirit, the presbytery, and the patrons of science, infidels and all, concur in attesting an ambassador of Christ, most assuredly we ought, with due submission, to sit at his feet. But this rebellious heart of mine wants something more than all the presbytery and the board of trustees can confer, in proof that . . . (he) is sent by the Holy Spirit, and a true ambassador of Jesus Christ. It is true that this sermon exhibits him very much in the true character of an ambassador, for as soon as an ambassador has proved his mission, his mere assertions and *say so's* are equal to all the logic and rhetoric of Demosthenes and Cicero united in one head. Consequently the Doctor, laying infinite stress upon his own infallibility, has not adduced one single scrap from Moses to John, to prove the subject of his discourse. This is, indeed, ambassador-like . . . (An ambassador) ought to *take no text at all*, but make a text for himself. The taking of a text implies inferiority and dependence, every way unbecoming "the legate of the skies."[2]

Did not the Pope of Rome claim a call? Where was the shade of difference?[3] These and other such inquiries provoked some,[4] but were received gratefully by others. Samuel Rogers of Ohio remembered how a heavy gloom hung over him when he would think of his call and compare it with that of the apostles. "Bless the Lord!," he cried "Alexander Campbell came to my relief."[5] Also from Ohio was another subscriber who appreciated the teaching regarding God's call. This one signing his letter with the lone initial "W." wrote: "this same *Christian Baptist* has stripped me of my "call," my "ambassadorship," *etc.* and has taught me that the treasure which the Apostles had in earthly vessels I have in the Bible; and, in a word, has left me simply a disciple and laborer in the vineyard in common with all others, according to our several abilities."[6]

From its first days of publication the *Christian Baptist* addressed the clergy and asked them to answer three questions: Have you heard God's voice? Do you speak infallibly? Can you confirm the testimony by working miracles?[7]

The miracle was a "must." The voice of Christ heard (not an inner feeling so interpreted) was essential in a call. Campbell gave this story:

Suppose this same man who contends for a call, without a voice, had a son ploughing in his field, and his son leaves the plough and goes to visit his friends. After some time he sends a message for his son. His son appears; and when asked why he forsook the plough, and went about riding and feasting with his friends, he answers, Father, you called me from the plough and commanded me to visit your and my friends. Nay, son, replies the father, did you hear my *voice calling* or *commanding* you to such a course of conduct? No, father, replies the son, I did not hear your voice specially calling or commanding me, but I had a deep impression on my mind that it was your wish and my duty to leave the plough and go avisiting. Go, sir, answers the irritated father, to your plough, and remember it is time enough to consider yourself called when you hear my voice.[8]

It was hard for Campbell to understand how a man with no pretence of a divine call, like Elder John Secrest, could report to immersing five hundred and thirty persons with his own hands in six months while many God-called preachers claiming an apostolic *succession* of sorts were experiencing no apostolic *successes*.[9] It was impossible for Campbell to believe that contradictory men as different as Swedenborg, Fox, Calvin, Wesley, or Gill,[10] could all be sent by God.

As to "speaking infallibly," it was noted that in his day some very ignorant men were making some exceedingly great claims at a divine call. Campbell pointed out that the "unlearned and ignorant" men that Christ had called did not continue ignorant after he called them but showed a wisdom beyond human learning. He pressed the observation: "when Christ called a blind man he opened his eyes, while our blind continue blind after the pretended call."[11]

To whom did Christ say the words recorded in Matthew 28:19-20 or Mark 16:15-16? Campbell replied:

I understand the commission as follows: "Go ye, Peter and Andrew, James and John, Zebedee, Philip and Bartholemew, Thomas and Matthew Levi; James Alpheus and Lebbeius Thaddeus, with Simon the Canaanite, and disciple all nations, immersing the believers of all nations into the faith of the Father, and of the Son, and of the Holy Spirit, teaching the baptized disciples to observe all things whatsoever I have commanded you, either before or since my resurrection from the dead—and take notice that I shall be ever present, with signs and wonders, to confirm your testimony, to the end of this state; for before this generation shall have passed away the gospel shall be preached to all nations for a testimony to them"[12]

The apostles of Christ still were going into all the world through their writings. "Though dead, they still preach,"[13]

Campbell reasoned. Like "Moses was preached being *read* in the synagogues," the apostles still published the news about Christ when their testimony was read.[14] As the law and the prophets prophesied until John, Christ and the apostles continued testifying in all ages. Their supernatural works "were *written* for the same purpose they were wrought."[15] Only a new gospel would need a new group of especially called men to publish it and modern-day miracles to establish it.

In denying the special, divine call of the clergy, Campbell did not mean that there was no call at all, and therefore the Lord's people had nothing to do for him. There was rather a general call of Christ through the written word[16] to the total church. The mischief of a clergy was that "everybody's mouth was shut up but their own.[17] Campbell wrote: "I hold that every citizen in Christ's kingdom is bound to take up arms for the king, as much as I am; and if he cannot go to fight the battles of the Lord, he must take care of the wives and children of those who can, and who will fight for their king and country."[18]

The service of Christ was no monopoly of the clerical few who claimed special endowments. It was the work of all followers of Christ to the extent of their ability. "Competency to instruct, and the need for it" was the only call for preaching in its widest sense.[19] Six hundred thousand well-armed militia was better, in Campbell's view, than ten thousand regulars. He predicted:

I know from a little experience, and from some observation, as well as from what the Acts of the Apostles teach, that the most efficient system, ever yet adopted, was that of the Founder of the Christian institution of making every man and woman in the ranks *a preacher* in the ancient import of that term. Every church on his plan was a theological school—every Christian, a missionary; and every day's behavior, a sermon either in word or deed . . . This is a prominent part of the Reformation now needed; and it will be then, and not till then, when all the citizens of the kingdom of Heaven are *citizen soldiers*, that the armies of the aliens can be completely routed.[20]

Proper decorum, however, demanded avoiding mob rule wherein anyone and everyone at an assembly talked either at once or in rotation.[21] Decency and order looked beyond the private preaching and teaching of Christians to public preachers and teachers called by the church.[22] The entire church was given the general call to evangelize, baptize and catechize; as the apostles were given the special call from Christ. The church could and ought to pick from its midst qualified men whom they would call to some service as bishop, deacon, or preacher.[23]

Alexander Campbell's preaching-father, Thomas Campbell, had hoped for Alexander to preach someday.[24] But was this the desire of the heavenly Father? In December of 1811 young Campbell reviewed the hand of Providence over his life which suggested his obligation to a special devotion of life to Christ. He enumerated God's provisions to him of religious parents, a Christian wife, extraordinary deliverance with his life on two occasions, the talents and education equipping him to edify others, his desire for the salvation of himself and others, and God's giving him "a call from the church to preach the Gospel."[25] On January 1, 1812, by the authority of the single and tiny congregation at Brush Run (some eight miles southwest of Washington, Pennsylvania) where he had preached his first sermon in America in May, 1810, Alexander Campbell was ordained to the ministry of preaching and teaching. "Ordination" did not qualify Campbell for an office. It put him into an office for which the congregation believed him to be qualified.

There was something humbling in the "lay ministry," "no clergy" concept. And humility was an essential quality for the public servants of the church. Vanity was a beguiling temptation to preachers everywhere. The clergy "have occupied a most conspicuous place in the Egyptian, Chaldean, Persian, Grecian, Roman, and Anti-Christian empires," observed Campbell. The man destined for "holy orders," finally acquiring the coveted "Doctor of Divinity," in the process may become susceptible to pride. Campbell noted:

. . . my young priest gradually assumes a sanctimonious air, a holy gloom overspreads his face, and a pious sedateness reigns from his eyebrows to his chin. His very tone of voice participates in the deep devotion of his soul. His words flow on with a solemn slowness, and every period ends with a heavenly cadence. There is a kind of angelic demeanor in his gait, and a seraphic sweetness in all his movements. With his Sunday coat, on a Sabbath morn, he puts on a mantle of deeper sanctity, and imperceptibly learns the *three* grand tones —the Sabbath tone, the pulpit tone, and the praying tone—these are the devout, the more devout, and the most devout.[26]

Modesty and not arrogance ought to be the mark of the preacher. He should never be guilty of assuming an air as many had. "Egotism—A Few Hints to Some Preachers," an article by Archippus found room in the pages of the *Millennial Harbinger*[27] to ward off the enemy among those dedicated to the recovery of first century Christianity. Their buildings and their public spokesmen were to be "plain and unadorned, save with simplicity and neatness."[28] Their dress was not to be in keeping with that which was popular among seminaries during the twelfth and thirteenth centuries and which imbibed the "spirit of Popedom." It was rather to be that reflecting the humble spirit of the first century messengers of Christ.

From Europe, where so much pomp was evident to the
traveler from the American frontier, he wrote:

I blame not Kings and Queens for royal robes and vest-
ments—the bridegroom or the bride for a wedding garment; but to see . . . Bachelors and Doctors of Divinity, in apparel so theatrically vain and foolish—scarfed
and cassocked, gowned and tasseled, hooded and sash-
ed, caps the climax of learned folly and sainted pride.[29]

Like the farmer, editor, evangelist, teacher, mechanic,
merchant and postmaster that he was, Alexander Campbell
wanted to be known by his name alone and not by the
title Reverend, Bishop or even Mister.[30] He wanted the
preachers to think of their themes and their audiences rather
than themselves. Those speakers who were too conscious of
their delivery were to beware of becoming like men looking
into a mirror admiring themselves. While Campbell's ad-
mirers saw in him "the total absence of any disposition to
self-applause," remarking that he was "insensible to flattery,"[31]
an occasional enemy thought that few persons had ever
possessed more of the qualities of a religious demagogue"
than he and that he was "fond of public notoriety."[32]

In "An Address Delivered Before the Ohio State Missionary Society, at Its Anniversary, May 21, 1862," he
raised the "practical and all interesting question: What are
the qualifications and characteristics of the Evangelist, or
gospel preacher?"[33] One answer, besides that of true humility,
was that of prayerful earnestness. For the exception of an
article by debate-opponent N. L. Rice in the *Presbyterian
Exposition* (Louisville, January 5, 1857) charging Campbell
with monetary motives, this claim is never heard. Campbell
never ceased denouncing hirelings who preached for the pay
in it.[34] He, himself, had turned down "most generous offers"
by New York churches because of "having resolved at that
early day never to accept a salary for preaching."[35] It was
a stroke of humor when in 1828 he offered to give "the Rev.

Mr. Smith, of Kentucky" all his salary received for preaching during the last fifteen years of his life, if Mr. Smith could prove a certain charge.[36] It was a stroke of good fortune when he married into sufficient wealth to make such a self-giving ministry possible.

Christian "overseers" had a divine right to the financial support of the brethren when they called for it. Campbell just chose to preach without pay, as did Paul in apostolic times and as did many pioneer lay-preachers in frontier times. He was not remiss in raising funds for Christian professors at Bethany, the college of which he was founder and first president. His tour notes often included place, subject of sermon and amount raised for the school. He even allowed tickets of admission to be sold in St. Louis for a series of his lectures, with all funds going to the church there.[37] He exhorted brethren in the political centre, Columbus, to "purchase a lot . . . build a large tabernacle, and station an evangelist there who can command the attention of that community."[38]

Campbell filled another requisite characteristic of the preacher by having an earnest, prayerful life. No counterfeit was possible here. More attention by every preacher to the spirit of prayer, rather than to a fine style, would have suited him. His wife spoke of his consistent life of "fervent, ardent prayer, constantly in the family and in the closet." She broke into exclamation when she thought of the prayers she had heard, including many he had uttered at the midnight hour "whilst profoundly asleep."[39]

Inseparably connected with the pastoral quality of prayerful earnestness was that of morality and wisdom. The *Harbinger* series on "Ministerial Character," stated that "a deep and sublime piety, a pure and noble morality on the part of the minister of the gospel, with a reasonable amount of learning and utterance, is more than worth all the attainments of a Selden or an Erasmus, and all the eloquence of a Cicero or a Demosthenes, without these scriptural and divine accomplishments."[40]

The high qualities of a gospel minister that Campbell had copied in his journal during student days at Glasgow, had put piety first; and, after humility, being "well instructed in morality and religion, and in the original tongues in which the Scriptures are written."[41]

Piety was the greater eloquence. Without living the gospel life, the eloquence of Apollos would have been vain. Campbell wrote: "[Man's] influence never can precede, but must, in the order of things, depend upon, and follow after character."[42] The "sage of Bethany," being of good heart and clear understanding, gave weight to his teachings by the consistency of a life well-lived.

In the title of Editor Perry Epler Gresham's *Alexander Campbell, The Sage of Bethany: A Pioneer in Broadcloth* is a combined emphasis on the characteristics of intellect and dignity for which Campbell was noted and upon which Campbell insisted in every public messenger of the church. Campbell was a gentleman—a Southern Gentleman—and was very much at home among gentlemen. He quoted Cowper (Task—Book II) with full agreement in his attack on a minister's lightness of speech:

'Tis pitiful
To court a grin, when you should win a soul;
To break a jest, when pity would inspire
Pathetic exhortation; and t' address
The skittish fancy with facetious tales,
When sent with God's commission to the heart!
So did not Paul. Direct me to a quip
Or merry turn in all he ever wrote,
And I consent you take it for your text.
Your only one, till sides and benches fall.
No: he was serious in a serious cause,

And understood too well the weighty terms,
That he had ta'en in charge. He would not stoop
To conquer those by jocular exploits,
Whom truth and soberness assail'd in vain.[43]

To lack gravity would be like a physician coming to a dying man in agony with an amusing tale rather than a sympathetic hand. He loved and respected "Racoon" John Smith but never sat easy in his presence when the beloved John was beset with the temptation to joke in a message. When John grew palsied and tremulous through the passing of time, Campbell noticed: "His gravity, also, appears in more successful conflict with a tendency or endowment almost irrepressible, to say things which, though savory and good, are often better adapted to elicit a smile than a tear, even from the most serious and devotional hearers."[44]

Campbell, unlike his more crude friend, John Smith, used only those analogies that would be acceptable completely to the most delicate. Different from his debate opponent, N. L. Rice, who frequently drew audience laughs, Campbell was never recorded to have received that kind of a response. The grand themes and solemn occasions would make a jest of "more offensive savor than Solomon's dead fly in the ointment of the apothecary."[45]

He who would teach others must be one whose head was "full of light" and whose heart was "full of love."[46] Christ could be preached successfully only when preached according to the spirit and temper of Christ. Thus truth was to be spoken in love. Persuasion, not denunciation, was the key to the human heart, and darkness was dispelled by light and not by an inveighing against it. The evangelist ought to delight in dwelling on the love of God rather than on the fire of hell.

It was evident to the skeptics who listened in Tammany and Concert Halls to Campbell's three discourses against Infidelity that here was a man reasoning with them because he liked them and wanted to share with them something he really believed. In a letter to Campbell from the Society of Moral Philanthropists, they thanked him for his "friendly" visit and for his adding "dignity to their hall." They expressed gratitude for his conciliatory attitude towards all skeptics in "appealing to them as men—as *honest men*, instead of treating them with contumely, as is the conduct of the Christian priesthood of New York."[47]

Some in "the Christian priesthood of New York" and elsewhere felt the pinch of Campbell's attack on clericalism and couldn't agree to any compliments given regarding his loving nature. They saw "harsh epithets and much sarcasm" and the going "beyond all the bounds of scripture allowance"[48] in rigidity and satire in his writings. He looked into his own heart and said:

An unsympathizing man is a monster in the form of humanity . . . No man can enter a pulpit with any sincere hope of success who does not endeavor to concentrate his whole energies—his conscience, his heart, his whole benevolence and every tender sympathy of his nature on perishing humanity. He must feel as a humane friend would feel on seeing his neighbor's house on fire.[49]

Campbell looked to the Bible for an answer to his questions about the man called "preacher." What was his call? What ought to be his character? The echoing answer seemed to be clear to him that the churches of Christ, in the name of God, were to put all Christians to that task whereto they were qualified, under the leadership of men whom they had found humble and sincere, godly and dignified, loving and wise. Such church-sent men were to be trained in the Scripture to understand: (1) the people to whom they spoke, and (2) the message which they would bring to their audiences.

V MANKIND AND MISSION
The Audience

Proverbially, counting sheep has been considered a way of inducing sleep. A shepherd of souls, however, has been startled awake occasionally upon counting his flock and realizing how many have strayed from the fold.

Campbell like all public speakers was not only cognizant of his subject but of the subjects before him—who they were? How many they were? Where they were religiously? In letters to his wife, in notes to his co-editors, or in diaries and other personal records, he wrote about the audiences that heard him.[1]

When on tour away from home, as he often was, the general difficulty was to find a building large enough to accommodate the people flocking from near and far. This meant in most cases asking for the use of the most commodious church in town, which very seldom was the building where the "disciples" gathered. The city hall, the county court-house, the open-air of a public square, the theatrical halls or debating halls of a city, the lecture rooms on a college campus or the railway station might suffice. Even when special facilities for the occasion were constructed in the open air, the crowds most always exceeded the estimations.[1]

Campbell in a court-house "found two square feet on the Judges bench" reserved for him, while the whole area was but "one compact mass of flesh and blood." In churches he addressed also the portion that could hear "through the windows."[2] In conventions he spoke with "as many thousands as could satisfactorily hear the voice of one man." His notes repeated like a broken record that in city after city he had delivered a certain number of addresses to "large and attentive auditories," "to one of the largest assemblies I have ever seen in that city,"[3] to "the largest congregation we had till then addressed east of the Blue Ridge,"[4] "to immense auditories in the largest Hall in this city,"[5] *etc.*

Mark Twain told of Campbell's coming to Hannibal, Missouri and of the excitement among the farmers who came from miles around to get a glimpse of him.

> When he preached in a church, many had to be disappointed, for there was no church that would begin to hold all the applicants; so in order to accommodate all, he preached in the open air in the public square, and that was the first time in my life that I realized what a mighty population this planet contains when you get them all together.[6]

As a convention speaker, Campbell addressed throngs of eager listeners. The early sermon that instigated much of his future course, the historic "Sermon on the Law," was delivered to the combined representatives of thirty-three Baptist churches in the Redstone Baptist Association. More than a thousand were in attendance with some twenty-two preachers.[7] In his growing popularity it was not long until, like in the 1839 yearly meeting of the reformers in Cuyohoga County of Ohio, the audience was more than five thousand.[8]

Even in Europe where a "Disciples' meeting house" might contain eight hundred at the morning worship hour on the Lord's Day, twenty-five hundred would gather in the evenings of the week at a larger hall.[9] Hundreds were said to have left upon such occasions, finding no admission possible.[10] More than once alarm was expressed that over-crowded galleries might collapse.[11] Campbell made the sage observation regarding those engaged in the nineteenth century reformation:

> The ears of the people are greedy; and were the desire to do equal to the desire to know, we would certainly be the most exemplary people in the world.[12]

Nothing dampened the ardor of the "Christians only" unless it was the disagreeable rain that in some areas came down with enough vehemence to cut into the attendance of a people that walked or drove a horse-carriage miles to the meeting. Enthusiastic requests for Campbell's visit promised: "rain or shine, we should be thronged.[13] The agreement was kept most of the time. It is understandable, however, when W. K. Pendleton had to record "The evening . . . rainy, the audience small, and the discourse admirable."[14]

The size of Campbell's audiences was not as significant as their makeup. In spreading the message of reform, Campbell did not forget the principles enunciated in the "Declaration and Address" which affirmed that the church was "essentially, intentionally and constitutionally one," and that his co-workers, while "Christians only," were not the only Christians. To his meetings came preachers and other Christians from most all the major sects. He had been the defender of the total Christian cause in a debate with the skeptic Robert Owen and the champion of all Protestant-Christianity when he engaged the Roman Bishop (later Archbishop) Purcell.

In community after community the denominational churches were open to him—Methodist, Presbyterian, Baptist, Unitarian, Episcopal, Universalist, and the "good 'auld Kirk o' Scotland." Even the "Jerusalem Temple" (i.e. synagogue) was offered him as a platform.[15] Human nature being what it was and clerical jealousy being a possibility, it was not unthinkable when the rare record appeared: "We found the

Presbyterian, Methodist, and Baptist churches locked up, and St. Peter in possession of the keys."[16]

Besides being often interdenominational in texture, the audience of Campbell was occasionally interracial. Sometimes he spoke with entirely Negro congregations.[17] At other times he taught a mixed audience in "separate but equal" facilities, although in the same room. In Louisiana the record was kept:

> A considerable colored population attended our meeting there, to whom was allotted one entire range of pews from the pulpit to the door, while the white population occupied three ranges of pews of the same length. The seats of both classes were alike cushioned, and no difference appeared, excepting the more fervent devotion.[18]

There were other forms of partial segregation at that time. In some places in what Campbell termed "Methodistic style" young ladies were divided from the young men.[19] In other places, due entirely to circumstances, husbands and families were separated as gentlemen gave their seats to the ladies and retired to stand outside a door or window.[20]

Another interesting fact about the crowd that hurried to hear Campbell was neither the age and sex mixture, racial mixture, nor religious mixture, but the coming together of men of no education and those of the highest education. Lawyers and judges came to witness his extraordinary dialectic power, schooled clerics to gain an advanced learning in scriptural studies, presidents and cabinet members to hear a reasonable presentation of the gospel.[21] Teachers, physicians, editors, men of intellect came to be stimulated by one of the finest minds of the nineteenth century. And, yet, the common people heard him gladly. As D. S. Burnet reminisced before Bethany College at the loss through death of their President: "the stream flowed on until every little goblet and great vase . . . was filled."[22]

In this chapter we have dealt to this point with the audience as it appeared to the physical eye. To a biblically saturated mind, such as Campbell's, what was perceived beyond what the eye could see? In the variety of people congregated, what was the common nature of man as man? The preacher must understand the man to whom he spoke before he could understand his mission to mankind.

While the politician regards man rather as a subject of taxation; the merchant, as an article of trade; the naturalist, as a mere animal, governed by appetite and passion; while each profession regards him in reference to itself; the physician, as a *patient*; the lawyer as a *client*; the priest, as a *tithable*; the Christian preacher regards him as God's prodigal son, the fallen child of his love; as yet capable of immortality under a remedial constitution, and his soul travails for his salvation. He remembers what he once was, and well he knows that the faith which has purified his heart and enabled him to overcome the world . . . can transform another lion into a lamb, another raven into a dove.[23]

For a prodigal to be brought home from the far country, he needs someone to lead him to a restoration of his senses. He must be made to think. One Elijah with convincing evidence was considered more effective than four hundred and fifty prophets of Baal who vociferously might wear out their lungs and zealously spill their blood to win an allegiance to their cause. The Christian gospel was a message from the mind of God to the mind of man. Enlightening the human understanding was "God's chartered way to the heart."[24] The model sermons in the book of Acts were not enthusiastic appeals to the passions. They were devoid of "declamation, noise, tinselling, painting, and mincing" and were all "logic, reason, point, testimony, proof."[25]

Men were to be appealed to through their intellects and brought back to good, common-sense. A sermon's purpose was to instruct and convince with irresistible logic. It was to tell the hearer why the speaker believed in, and loved the Lord Jesus. Campbell argued:

All who either tell or proclaim in a pulpit or on a chair, their own convictions and feelings, doubts, fears, and hopes, preach themselves or their feelings, instead of Jesus Christ. I presume a pious Mussulman could narrate his feelings, doubts, extacies (*sic*), and joys in "the Prophet Mahomet (*sic*)." But he who could expect to convert others to any faith by such a course, calculates very largely upon the ignorance and weakness of his audience. All evidences are addressed to the higher and more noble faculties of man. The understanding, and not the passions, is addressed; and therefore an appeal to the latter, before the former is enlightened, is as unphilosophic as it is unscriptural. As the helm guides the ship, and the bridle the horse, so reason is the governing principle in man. Now in preaching Jesus arguments are to be used—and these are found in the testimony of God. To declare that testimony, and to adduce the evidences which support it, is to proclaim the gospel.[26]

In this quotation we notice that an appeal to the passions "before" the understanding was addressed was what Campbell considered "unphilosophic" and "unscriptural." An appeal to emotion was to be subsidiary to intellectual appeal. Otherwise a man's faith would be founded not on solid rock but on a balloon—upon feeling and imagination. The legitimate role of the feelings was to ignite—as a spark ignites a fire—the carefully laid facts that had been placed log-like in the mind. A sermon in Campbellian style would be a clear statement of forceful reasons for believing in Jesus as Christ and savior, followed with a fervent appeal to commit one's life to him. As Campbell remarked during the Owen debate:

When men have reasoned very strongly and carried a point by a very powerful attack upon the human understanding, they may be allowed to slacken the reigns upon the passions, and make some appeal to the hearts or feelings of the audience.[27]

Good preaching, in Campbell's book, steered the course between Calvinism which aimed "too much at the head" and Arminianism that addressed too much "the passions." Good preaching followed the apostolic gospel which simultaneously addressed "the understanding, the conscience, and the heart."[28] While Campbell was not as emotional in his teaching as the communities were used to and many individuals wished; he wanted the record clear that he was not against the *emotion* that led to *devotion*. He opposed the *all-emotion* that, under revivalists, produced a *commotion*. This caused men to howl, tremble and jump, or dogs to bark, children to cry, birds to sing and sinners to tremble.[29] He wrote:

> Let no one hence infer that we are opposed to feeling. God forbid! A religion without feeling is a body without a spirit. A religion that does not reach the heart and rouse all our feelings into admiration, gratitude, love and praise, is a mere phantom. But we make feelings the *effect*, not the *cause* of faith and of true religion. We begin not with feelings, but with the understanding; we call upon men first to believe, then to feel, and then to act. The gospel takes the whole man —the head, the heart, the hand; and he only is a genuine Christian who believes, feels, and obeys from the heart the whole mould of doctrine delivered to us by the holy Apostles.[30]

It is true that Campbell was not boisterous in the pulpit. Nevertheless, he spoke with "an earnestness often rising into impassioned utterance."[31] His sermon notes and editorials were frequently marked with exclamation points and proved to be devotional exercises as well as reasons and arguments. A man as sedate as Henry Clay (and as determined as he was, being debate moderator, to avoid the appearance of favoring one debater over the other) was so captivated by the reasoned argument of Campbell that he leaned forward, bowed assent and waved approval.[32] Dr. Heman Humphrey, former President of Amherst College, upon hearing Campbell quote the twenty-fourth Psalm ("Lift up your heads, O ye gates") said, "I cannot, in justice refrain from acknowledging that I never remember to have listened to, or to have read a more thrilling outburst of sacred eloquence."[33] As a hearer, Campbell himself, could be moved emotionally. He shouted "Glory to God in the highest!" as he listened to Walter Scott's oration in a grove near Wheeling, Virginia.

The nature of the mission to bring man to faith and build him up in that faith, was determined by the nature of man and how he came to belief. Faith, to Campbell, was nothing but the belief in the testimony of credible witnesses. It came only "by receiving the testimony of another as true."[34] In the words of Paul faith came "by hearing." As you could not see without light, you could not believe without testimony. Any human being that could think could believe. In the place of bewilderment, darkness and mystery regarding a faith miraculously placed in the heart by the Holy Spirit's unpredictable working; Campbell substituted the dependable observation that as testimony to an event followed that event, faith in the witness borne, came after a well authenticated testimony. Almost all our knowledge of anything past or present was derived in man by faith in testimony. Campbell said, "Testimony is only another name for the experience of others."[35]

Christianity as a revelation had to do with the incarnation, an event of history. Like any other historical happening in time and space, eye-witnesses had called to our attention certain facts about Jesus—his birth, person, offices, mission, words and works. We could assent intellectually to a dogma, a proposition, a theory or a speculation. We might either believe or disbelieve testimony and obey or disobey precepts.[36] All history was testimony. It was the narrative of what happened. It was to events or facts that testimony was borne. Therefore, it was not the believing of a man that had saving power, it was that in which he believed.[37]

Evangelical Protestantism in Campbell's time distinguished "historic faith" from "saving faith." Campbell saw faith to be all of one kind:

> That error is, that the nature or power and saving efficacy of faith is not in the truth believed, but in the *nature* of our faith, or in the *manner of believing* the truth. Hence all that unmeaning jargon about the nature of faith, and all those disdainful sneers at what is called "historic faith"—as if there could be any faith without history, written or spoken. Who ever believed in Christ without hearing the history of him . . . Faith never can be more than the receiving of testimony as true.[38]

> The all-permeating and prevailing idea in *secular* and *sectarian* Christendom, seems to be,—that right *thinking*, right *feeling*, right *believing* are paramount and all-engrossing concerns, not seeming to recognize that the illuminating, sanctifying, regenerating influence is not in the act of believing, feeling, or thinking,—but in the *fact, act, event, person or thing accredited—perceived, received, and relied upon.*[39]

Christian faith was faith in a person—"a hearty reliance upon the Lord Jesus Christ for that salvation which he came into the world and died upon the cross to procure for lost sinners,"[40]—a confidence in a person, the admiration of a person, and a sincere devotion to his will."[41] Examination of the evidence was all God asked and all that was necessary to faith. But to exhort men to believe "without submitting evidence" would be as "absurd as to try to build a house or plant a tree in a cloud."[42]

Was this, in fact, leaving out the Holy Spirit in the conversion process? It was rather obviating the way by which

God worked "faith in the heart by his Holy Spirit" through "the belief of testimony."[43] He affirmed that "in conversion and sanctification the Spirit of God" operated "only through the Word of Truth."[44] In opposition to those who preached the Holy Spirit, rather than preaching Christ through the use of the sword of the Spirit, Campbell plead:

> To hear many of the moderns, who profess to preach *the word*, talk of it as they do, and represent it as a *dead* and inefficient letter, is enough to provoke the meekness of a Moses, or to awaken the indignation of a Paul. The voice of God spoke the universe into being from the womb of nothing. The same voice recreates the soul of man, and the same voice will awaken the dead at the last day. His voice, heard or read, is equally adapted to the ends proposed. Some look for another call, a more powerful call than the written gospel presents. They talk of an inward call, of hearing the voice of God in their souls. But what greater power can the voice of God in the soul have, or what greater power can this inward call have, than the outward call, or the voice of God, echoed by the Apostles? God's voice is only heard now in the gospel. The gospel is now the only word of God, or will of God—the only proclamation and command addressed to the human race. 'Tis in this word of God his Spirit operates upon men and not out of it.[45]

The Christian mission was to bring men to trust in Christ —to have confidence in him as a person. This goal was reached through testimony—the testimony of the apostles, presently recorded in the New Testament Scriptures. The Holy Spirit used that witness to bring about the change in man essential to his salvation. As certainly as testimony preceded faith, fruit followed it. Religious affections sprang from faith.

Campbell illustrated this with the grief that might come upon the learning of a friend's drowning. The order was:

the drowning, then the report of it to another, then the belief of the report, and finally the grief at that point of belief. From cause to effect, it was fact, testimony, belief, grief. There could be no exceptions to that order. In preaching to the world there was "a proper beginning and a proper ending." He affirmed that "The order of things in this philosophy is, first, the testimony of God; then, faith in that testimony; then, repentance; then, baptism and prayer; then, peace, and hope and joy, and love, then, all good works.[46] This means that preaching was an address to man's understanding in which the speaker narrated the wonderful works of God in Christ. He stated, illustrated and proved the gospel facts. He testified not only to what God had done, but to what he had promised and threatened. He persuaded the hearers to surrender to the guidance and direction of God's Son. The man of the world needed only to hear the gospel. This gospel had the power to produce faith, to bring assurance of divine favor, and to produce the reformation of life.

Faith to bear holy fruit had to be faith in Christ. The preaching that produced faith in Christ was the preaching of the gospel of Christ. Campbell was disturbed by his critics who thought the preaching of the Holy Spirit was preaching Christ and that Campbell was derelict for not, in every sermon, telling how bad he once was and how good he had become. That kind of preaching, Campbell felt, pointed the hearer's mind within to his own heart, rather than to Jesus the author of salvation. Preaching about the gospel—even on such themes as repentance, baptism, remission of sins and eternal life was not preaching the gospel—even as a medical lecture on a certain cure was not the same as offering the medicine. Preaching "faith" was not proclaiming "*the* faith." Aiming at a reform in dress and manners was not effecting the change of views, affections, state and life that constituted conversion. Getting the hearers to fall in love with a peculiar religious system, was not inducing sinners to give themselves up to Jesus.

The man who came within the preacher's voice range was to be reached through the mind by the sufficient evidence in the Scriptures. Whoever called on the name of the Lord would be saved; but the calling would follow believing, and the believing would commence at hearing, and preaching would initiate it all if it was the preaching of Christ to an unbelieving world.

But, said the Reformer:

So long as the notion obtains that clergymen are created, made, and ordained to dispense ordinances, to *Christen infants*, to *confirm children*, to marry adults, to *dispense the sacrament*, to pray for the sick, to preach funeral sermons, and march in funeral processions—to be Chaplains to armies, navies, and parliaments, and to write and pronounce sermons—we have infallible testimony that we are in the spiritual Babylonian Captivity.[47]

The messenger of the church had first to gaze at his audience to determine if he would be addressing prodigals or pupils—the world or the disciples of Christ. If the latter, he had to remember that the great commission admonished them to observe all that Christ commanded and that the epistles of the New Covenant were addressed to none other than baptized believers. If the unconverted were before him, the teacher of saints became the preacher to sinners and announced the gospel facts and promises for the single purpose of leading the lost to faith in Jesus as the Christ the son of the living God and into the Christian family.

VI MATTER AND MANNER
The Message

The druggist receives the physician's prescription. The pharmacist knows that he is to prepare the order using the precise ingredients in the exact amounts stated. It is not necessary to inform him that for this particular patient all the other drugs and medicines on the shelf are not to be included.

Campbell held that the single remedy for the world's ills, according to the prescription of the Great Physician, was the gospel. The shelves of Scripture were heavy-ladened with many truths prescribed for disciples, but the prescription for the world and that for the church were not to be confused.

To call for the preaching of the gospel to the unbelieving world limited every other consideration. This was important to recognize, for nothing else preached could have the redeeming effect of the gospel. Campbell believed that "When God, the omniscient, and the all-wise, selects any means for any end, reason must humbly bow to it as the best in the universe."[1]

To preach a creed was to take a "soul-alienating . . . discord-making . . . strife-breeding course" that would "scatter the seeds of discord throughout."[2] Preaching Christ brought men into the fold of Christ. Preaching a statement of faith led men into the fold of a party. The former saved.

64

The latter was impotent to convert sinners. As a matter of fact it had the effect of impeding the salvation of the world.

It was not good stewardship when a preacher used time, labor and money to prove that which, no matter how well proved, saved nor sanctified no man. Campbell reasoned:

This is, with us, the controlling reason, the sovereign consideration why we should not waste our lives in such South Sea dreams—why we should not cultivate barren sands on the sea border, while our fertile hills and rich alluvial vallies [*sic*] are undressed and unsown, and consequently unproductive in the good fruits of righteousness and life. What wise financier would invest his capital in the stock of broken companies, where he must ultimately lose, not only the interest, but the principal also! So is every one—preacher . . . who fills the ears and the hearts of those to whom he ministers with untaught and unprofitable questions . . . and inoperative speculations . . . He invests his labors in profit. He does worse than he who buried his talent in the earth; for in that case he might have saved the principal; but in this, both principal and interest are lost for ever.[3]

Orthodoxy was no high and holy ambition. Campbell declared Satan to be "as orthodox as Gabriel."[4] It was not preaching the gospel to declare another man's "orthodoxy" to be "heterodoxy." The preacher was no God-appointed juror to bring verdicts on another man's views. Aylett Raines, for example, was not to be excluded from the Mahoning Association because of his views regarding the "restoration" of all men, while at the same time he was not to be permitted to propagate a divisive opinion. Since the aim of all that message spoken to the world was their reconciliation to God, Campbell noted:

Proving tenets, exploding false theories or establishing the true, offering criticisms, discussing questions, resolving cases of conscience, or propounding principles of any sort, are no part of the work of converting sinners, or of preaching reformation to ungodly men . . . Therefore, conversion is a turning to the Lord—in order to which Christ must be preached, and nothing else.[5]

New Testament evangelists, like Philip, preached "Jesus." No theories of humanity nor of divinity were given. No doctrine of "total depravity" or of "regeneration" were argued. Christ was preached rather than a theory concerning Christ; a new life, and not a new formula of doctrine, was the world's need. "Christianity" was not Philip's theme; "Jesus" was. Also, to preach "regeneration" in order to produce regeneration was "as preposterous as the preaching of a resurrection in a graveyard to the ashes of the dead."[6]
Since the words of the Bible as well as the thoughts of the Bible were Holy Spirit guided, the preacher ought to be content with "the inspired symbols of evangelical ideas, as selected by the Spirit of wisdom and of revelation."[7] He ought to preach the gospel "as did the old Apostles, who were neither Calvinists, Arminians, Trinitarians, Unitarians, or any thing else but the followers of Christ."[8] Campbell reported:

There is something in the matter and manner of our preaching very different from any thing which we heard in Britain or Ireland . . . we begin at the day of Pentecost and speak from that book as if we had lived before Augustine, or Tertullian, or Origen, or Justin Martyr, or before the Protestant reformers were born.[9]

It was Campbell's desire that metaphysically-true dogmas, which came forth as distilled truths from Arminian and Calvinistic distilleries, be replaced by Christ's gospel in biblical terms. He hoped that schools of scholastic theology (where, in the words of a *Harbinger* contributor with the pen-name SILAS, there was preaching and prayer "as formal as a Quaker's coat, and as cold as December"[10]) would be replaced by Bible chairs in every college where the Scriptures would be taught as sacred history.

It is no wonder that if religious opinion was not the proper material for a gospel sermon, neither was political opinion. Campbell could care enough about social reform to be an active delegate to the (1829) Virginia convention called to amend the State constitution. Yet, when he preached every night during the three-month session in various churches in and near Richmond, his leftist political opinions were not even whispered from the pulpit. Campbell could argue against John Marshall and John Randolph as he dreamed of slavery's abolition. Yet, when in Montrose, Scotland, he could write his daughter Clarinda: "Some were super-excited, and came rather to hear us on the subject of American slavery than on the gospel. We did not, however, gratify them, having a paramount object in our eye."[11]

Campbell could plead before literary societies for the equal education of women and also for a universal education; yet, like Daniel Webster, he did not believe preachers should "take their texts from St. Paul and preach from the newspapers."[12] Campbell could see the "ignorance, poverty, and crime" abounding in the big cities.[13] But, he was convinced that the cure was not in turning "aside to electioneer for some great hero other than the Captain of our salvation."[14]

More than once the *Millennial Harbinger* told the story of Dr. Chalmer's experience in his pastorate at Kilmany and his determination for the next ministry in Glasgow. In Kilmany for twelve years he had preached against "the pests and disturbers of human society." He pressed reformation of every kind among his people. But, he said, "I never once heard of any such reformation having been effected among them." He became convinced of the utter alienation of the heart from God. He also found the subordinate reformations for which he had earlier preached, coming as the consequence of preaching Christ's free offer of forgiveness. He confessed: "I am now sensible that all the vehemence with which I urged the virtues . . . had not the weight of a feather on the moral habits of my parishioners." Campbell, agreeing with Chalmers, concluded that to preach Christ was the only effective way of teaching morality. "Morality," he insisted, was "a fruit of the gospel—of gospel reconciliation to God and men."[15]

Negatively considered, to preach the gospel was not to preach theories, opinions, creeds, politics, orthodoxy or even the Bible. Nor was it to preach the Law. The gospel did not rest for its effectiveness upon the Law being first preached. When Campbell preached his Sermon on the Law before the convention of Baptists, he lost many friends when, contrary to the popular view, he insisted that there was "no necessity for preaching the law in order to prepare men for receiving the gospel."[16] The great commission assigned the task of preaching the gospel, not the Law. The apostles were constituted ministers of the New Testament, not the Old. The Book of Acts gave in all its sermons the approved precedent of preaching only the gospel and not an instance of preparing Jew or Gentile by lawpreaching.

The Holy Spirit of Truth was to convict the world of sin, righteousness and judgment, not through the Law of Moses but through the testimony of Christ. Campbell taught:

The eternal Father condemned sin in the person of his Son, more fully than it ever was, or could be, condemned in any other way. Suppose, for illustration, a king put to death his only son, in the most painful and ignominious way, for a crime against the government: would not this fact be the best means of convincing his subjects of the evil of the crime, and of the king's detestation of it? Would not this fact be better than a thousand lectures upon the excellency of the law and the sanctions of it?[17]

At this teaching the Baptists protested that to follow Campbell at this point was heretical, licentious and "antinomian." To this he replied: "Blessed Jesus! art thou thus insulted by pretended friends? Are thy laws an inadequate rule of life? Guided by thy statutes will our lives be licentious, our morals loose, ourselves abandoned to all crime?"[18]

Positively speaking, preaching the gospel was preaching Jesus—"his Divine and human personality, his official splendors, his august titles, his personal charms, his condescending grace and loveliness."[19] Gospel proclamation was "the simple declaration of the great facts of redemption—the things that man had done in his rebellion—and what God has done to redeem him."[20] It then enjoined upon man new precepts that grew out of these facts with promises accompanying. "There are gospel facts to be believed—gospel precepts to be obeyed—and gospel promises to be enjoyed and hoped for—and a Saviour, to be loved, admired, and served."[21]

Seven facts constituted the whole gospel, Campbell taught, referring to the birth, life, death, burial, resurrection, ascension, and coronation of Christ. The facts about his "person, mission, sacrifice and intercession"[22] were renovating in power. Concerning these facts the world needed to be informed, convinced and then exhorted to decide regarding Christ. The preacher's task was to produce the evidence that Jesus was the Son of God and the savior of sinners. To help other preachers at this task Campbell designed a brief volume, *The Christian Preacher's Companion or The Gospel Facts Sustained by the Testimony of Unbelieving Jews and Pagans.*[23] This book grew out of Campbell's own work at the preaching task. He often reasoned with skeptics to their enjoyment, and many times to their conversion.

Upon faith *in* Christ, reformation (or repentance) *toward* Christ and immersion *into* Christ, the convert was ready for teaching concerning all that Christ expected of him as a follower. While the preacher's message was as single as the gospel, the Christian teacher's topics were as broad as, but no more broad than, the Scriptures. To occupy the teacher were all the meanings of the gospel facts, all the implications of a life in Christ, all the rules for work and worship in the epistles, all the information for our admonition from Adam to Moses, from Moses to the Messiah, and from Matthew to John. These were proper topics for the comfort and edification of the church.

The teaching was to be more practical and exhortatory than explanatory and exegetical. If Campbell's own teaching can be considered any standard for others, each teaching was to be viewed against the backdrop of the whole biblical revelation. Campbell had the reputation for perceiving the "vital principles of revelation in wide and expanded views."[24] He would not exhaust a phrase or a word. His sermons had scope and dimension. In the words of his biographer: "His grand generalizations of the wonderful facts of redemption opened up trains of reflection wholly new, and presented the subject of Christianity in a form so simple and yet so comprehensive as to fill everyone with admiration.[25]

Campbell was at the opposite pole from those "textuaries" who analyzed the words of a phrase with no attention to their place in a given book or in the Bible as a whole. On one occasion Campbell listened for forty-five minutes to a Presbyterian cleric, Dr. Blair, speaking on the line "Why will ye die, O house of Israel!" Campbell calculated the speaker's salary per sermon and concluded that, if that phrase of a verse cost the congregation twenty-six dollars, it would take $1,300,000 and a thousand years to have the entire Bible explained to them.[26]

Whether a servant of the church was addressing men in the kingdom of darkness or the kingdom of light, the way of speaking would have a similarity even though the content would be dissimilar. In both confrontations Campbell believed the style should be conversational.

Riding along with "Racoon" John Smith, Campbell listened to Smith's observation of his preaching style: "You leaned upon your cane easily, though somewhat awkwardly, and talked as men commonly talk." Campbell replied that although he had studied the arts of elocution, he conscientiously refrained from their use. Then he pointed Smith to the apostolic manner: "Suppose that one of them should . . . have plied his arms in gesticulations, stamped his foot in vehemence, and declared his testimony . . . in a loud, stentorian voice?" Rather, Campbell said, there was "composure of manner, natural emphasis, and solemn deliberation."[27]

In the New Testament examples of preaching where men "so spake" that many hearers believed, the manner was not that of declamation. There was "no pomp nor pageantry of language—no fine lights of fancy—no embellishments of the rhetorical character."[28] There was "no effort to soften the heart by melting tones, gentle cadences, or an impassioned mannerism."[29]

One learned to speak by speaking, and in Campbell's daily routine there were constant conversations with family, student body and friends. As he one time remarked, "Reading makes an intelligent man—writing a correct man—conversation a fluent man."[30] Campbell did read widely, he did write carefully and he did talk constantly. Always the voice was conversational whether talking to a large congregation or at an informal gathering around the hearth. Never was there a preaching-tone in the former situation and another tone for the latter occasion. He ridiculed divines who supposed that their tone of voice should differ from that of lawyers, states-men and lecturers since in the cleric's opinion a sacred sub-ject demanded a sacred tone. He assured young preachers that "true gracefulness and dignity in a speech" was to be found in "the natural tone" and "the natural key."[31]

As one might expect, conversational preaching, to Camp-bell, had the air of dialogue, not monologue. He encouraged audience participation; and, besides anticipating questions that he answered in the sermons, he often allowed for ques-tion and answer periods either immediately following the message or at the next opportunity. In this he followed the same principles as he had in the *Millennial Harbinger* where he permitted arguments for and against all his positions to be heard. It was his conviction that teaching Christ, like teaching all other subjects, was more effectively accomplished through teacher-pupil conversation. He included in his jour-nal an article to this point by a contributor who signed his work with the initial "N." "If a professor of any other science than the science of religion were to pretend to in-struct his class merely by lecturing to it, he would be turned off as one that did but half his duty. The church, in this respect ought not to differ from the college."[32] Campbell's reform rested upon getting people to think for themselves. His defeat would be for the people to be persuaded by clerics to let clergymen do the thinking in religion for the members.

For a sermon to be truly conversational, it ought, also, to be delivered in an extemporaneous manner. In the beginning of Campbell's ministry, following standards he had set for himself, he wrote a sermon (three to be exact) in full and committed it to memory. When later he committed himself to the Bible standard for method of delivery as well as mes-sage to be delivered, this all changed. What apostle read to those gathered his own sermon or one purchased from another? Would Peter have been speechless if one day his sermon had been misplaced in the saddlebag? Could Paul not have prayed with the Ephesian elders at Miletus, if the written prayer in his pocket had been lost?

Extemporaneous speaking was more than biblical, it was the superior mode of speaking.

Our words react upon ourselves according to their importance, and hence, we are sometimes wrought up to a pathos, a fervor, an ecstasy, indeed, by the mysterious sound of our own voice upon ourselves, as well as that of others, to which we never could have ascended without it. Hence the superior eloquence of extemporaneous speaking over that of those who read or recite what they have cooly (*sic*) or deliberately thought at some time and in some other place.[33]

Describing his shift from the writing and memorization of sermons to the freedom of talking freely to the audience, Campbell said that in his first efforts in the pulpit he "felt as embarrassed as one corseted." He sensed being cramped. In his second and third attempts he had a few notes and interspersed extemporaneous comments between what he had written. This brought the sense of putting a new patch on an old garment, making the rent worse. From then on, while his messages were well prepared in the organization of his thought, they were entirely extemporaneous.

Campbell had an aversion both to writing sermons and to reading them to the public. Yet how much worse it would be to hide the written sermon in a Bible or a black book the size of the Bible. This would lead the hearers to believe the lie that no notes were used. Such would be unbecoming. This he called "Pulpit Dishonesty," in an article for his paper, *The Christian Baptist*.[34] You would not read a manuscript in conversation to friends in the parlor. Why, then, not talk face to face, eye to eye and heart to heart with the audience of sinners or saints.

Only the determination to speak as the apostles spoke, plus the gift of a very capable memory, allowed Campbell to address men extemporaneously. His sermons on a tour were of one and a half to three hours in length. Not many, if any, could do what Campbell did in the information-packed, twelve hour, extemporaneous, debate-speech against Robert Owen. Only important matter and an intriguing manner caused the auditors to think upon such occasions that they had listened to Campbell for no more than half-an-hour.

A conversational sermon must not be an effort at eloquence. By that very fact it cannot fail to be truly eloquent. The weapons of the world having no part in the armor of a Christian soldier, let the eloquence within the churches of Christ be an eloquence in scripture doctrine, in argument, in exhortation, in all good works.[35]

This was the brand of oratory Editor W. T. Moore saw in Campbell when he prepared the "dedication" for Campbell's *Familiar Lectures on the Pentateuch*, which began: "To the students of Bethany College, who have listened to the old man eloquent"[36] Campbell's eloquence was an art-less eloquence, for his every effort was only to be understood. His mind was on his subject and his object, not on himself.

After pooling together hints from contemporaries of Campbell in action, we see through their eyes and hear through their ears Campbell bringing an address:

His appearance is impressive, self-assuring and command-ing. He stands six-feet tall and is vigorous and masculine as hard outdoor work was certain to make him. His grey eyes flash out from beneath heavy brows and pierce deeply. His pleasant countenance radiates in contrast to the drab-colored suit he wears. His voice is clear and ringing, his tone deep and melodious; his enunciation precise; his Scotch-

Color-King Natural Color Card, Cline Photo, Inc., Chattanooga, Tenn

31947

oto by W.M. Cline Co.

POST CARD

Address

PLACE
STAMP
HERE

brogue with a Yankee strain not detracting. He speaks with such rapidity, he denies the best stenographers a complete and accurate record of all he says.[37] Yet, even the foreign terms, pompous phrases or heavy vocabulary, seem natural to him and not frustrating to us.

His words are vivid and well-chosen, though at times more extensive than his audience's ability to grasp. His figures of speech are primarily metaphors. His sentences are constructed properly and varied in both length and kind. His style seems an effort at plainness rather than embellishment. Any gestures of emphasis and description are noticeable by their absence, but they are unnecessary because of the strong emphasis he lays on important words and the exacting choice he has made of meaningful terms! He seems not to want the delivery of the message to call attention to itself. To him, the message is the all-important thing.

Among the items received from Australia was a cravat worn by Alexander Campbell, Jr. on his wedding day. Shown above is a picture of his father wearing a similar neckpiece.

The manuscript books received from Australia. The condition shown here indicated that much restoration and repair is necessary before any extensive use is made of them. At the left is a copy of Robert Richardson's The Principles and Objects of the Religious Reformation Urged by A. Campbell and Others which is inscribed "To A. Campbell with the Christian regard of R. R. June 14th 1853."

Manuscript D with its title "Journal of a Voyage from Ireland towards America, 1808," is self-explanatory. Like all of the manuscript books, the contents include much material not indicated in the title.

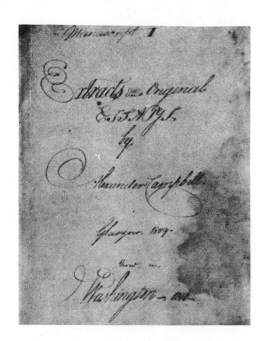

Title page of Manuscript 1, "Extracts and Original Essays by Alexander Campbell, Glasgow 1809, now in Washington, 1810."

The lower portion of a page from Manuscript E showing "Alexander Campbell in the 20th year of my age, being born on the 12th of September 1788 . . . Glasgow." It can be seen that he wrote 1888, crossed it out and then wrote in the correct year.

In an untitled record book showing money paid to various people by Alexander Campbell for the construction of Bethany College are additions made by Mrs. Campbell long after her husband's death. Shown here is a recipe for ginger snaps, copied from the Christian Moniter, March 13th 1882. Note the manner in which Mrs. Campbell initialed the item at the bottom of the page (Bethany Mansion, Mrs. A. C., Sr.).

The first item in the unlabeled note book is a sermon from Romans 6:14, "Ye are not under the law, but under grace." This shows Campbell's thinking in 1812 and a comparison with the famous "Sermon on the Law," 1816, should show his development in four years.

PART TWO

ALEXANDER CAMPBELL: PREACHER OF REFORM

VII MOLDS AND MODELS
Campbell's Background

Whoever sets up a standard *for* others subjects himself to the judgment *of* others as to whether he lived up
to his own high ideals. Paraphrasing Paul to the Romans
in our questions to Campbell, we ask: "You that taught
others, did you teach yourself? When you said not to
adulterate a gospel sermon with pagan Athenian eloquence,
were your teachings always chaste? You who forbade steal-
ing another's message from some sermon-book and killing
congregational interest by stumblingly reading it, are you
without blemish concerning these charges?"

Selina Huntington Campbell, in the book concerning her
husband's *Home Life* leads us to a major molding influence
upon Campbell. We have reason to suspect that, like many
a preacher's wife, the "help-meet" (with whom Alexander
shared his innermost thoughts and before whose offspring
he talked daily regarding eternal things) discussed with
him sermonic thoughts before and after their public hearing. There is definite trace in letters to her husband that
Selina had ideas about articles for the religious journal
edited by Mr. Campbell.

Long before Alexander Campbell left father and mother
to cleave to a wife, a home life of molding power was to
be found in the manse of Mr. and Mrs. Thomas Camp-

bell. Alexander loved and respected his Huguenot mother (Jane Corneigle) and Scottish father (Thomas Campbell). Their insistence that all children and domestics in their care were to memorize for recitation at least one Bible verse a day was, according to Alexander's confession, a dominating factor in making him what he was. From his lips could flow not only chapters, but entire books of the Bible. Scriptural terminology was indelibly stamped into his mind.

Thomas Campbell was a capable and respected preacher in the Psalm-singing, Scotch Seceder Presbyterian Church. He followed with precision their homiletical rules. His son, Alexander, heard from him substantial preaching. In later years, after the son began to preach, the two of them would walk and talk all the way home from a church service testing each other's message for content, composition and arrangement according to the clerical standards of the Scotch Seceder ministry. The doctrine was to be that of the text and the divisions of the speech were to exhaust the subject. Alexander would not have felt robbed as had Philip (only signature used) writing in the *Christian Baptist*: "I have spent twenty years of my life under the noisy verbosity of a Presbyterian clergyman without receiving the least degree of light from the Holy Word of God."[1]

Once Alexander had committed his life to the ministry, Thomas charted the course of preparatory study, insisting upon at least six months of a most intensive study of the Bible. While Alexander was not to neglect the study of other books, the one book in which he must of necessity be expert was the Bible. Until his death, Alexander made a daily personal searching of the Scriptures the essential element in the preacher's routine of life. Like father, like son—Alexander and Thomas both were biblical preachers; both generalized upon their topics and defined with brevity and accuracy the terms they used. Alexander, nevertheless, went beyond his revered father for his highest ideal of what preaching ought to be. In freeing himself from denominational patterns, he could see that his father's old sermon manuscripts showed occasional traces of "scrap preaching" in the "old way of . . . worthy ancestors"[2] rather than the better way of apostolic precedent.

Thomas Campbell was not only Alexander's father and preacher, he was also his instructor in such subjects as the Greek and Latin languages. When a shipwreck on the Island of Islay (Oct. 7, 1808) created the opportunity of studying a year at the University of Glasgow before continuing the journey to America, Alexander followed in his father's footsteps once again by enrolling as a student there and by supporting himself through giving private instruction in Latin, grammar and arithmetic. Robert Richardson, Alexander Campbell's biographer, sees the formative influence of the Glasgow teachers on him, especially George Jardine in Logic and Rhetoric and John Young in Greek, Grammar and Elocution.[3] The habit of rising at 4 a. m. to study and not retiring before 10 p. m. that started in Glasgow followed throughout his life. While he was at the University, Campbell had the further broadening experience of hearing preachers from various denominations and of enjoying with other students frequent pastoral interviews in their homes. It is likely that the writings of John Locke on toleration, human understanding and Christianity's reasonableness lodged in his thinking.

Campbell not only shared the education that travel brought to a preacher's family but continued to learn from the school of experience in later life. When he informed the readers of his journals about a recent tour across some section of America or to Europe, he brought out knowledge of the historical significance of the building where he spoke or the port from which he sailed. The subscribers to the *Millennial Harbinger* received a liberal arts education from a Christian viewpoint and rubbed shoulders through their editor with some of the great minds of the world. When Campbell would pay a visit to such as the House of Lords in London, he would bring back to his followers an evaluation of the speaking style of a Lord Brougham or some other. When he would hear a celebrated Congregational preacher like Dr. Raffles of Liverpool, or a Calvinist in Richmond, or fellow-disciples such as Walter Scott, D. S. Burnet, Jacob Creath, Isaac Errett, Sidney Rigdon, Peter Ainslie, or a host of others, he could not refrain from reacting like a professor of preaching to the substance, organization and delivery of their themes. If he did not run in his paper the entire sermon, he usually recorded the theme, audience response and his criticism of the message. These evaluations of other's sermons were for the edification of the public messengers among Campbell's readers, but they must also have shaped to some degree his own future efforts to speak more effectively for Christ. While he consciously tried to forget what he had learned in courses and books regarding the art of elocution, his remarks showed that he was never unconscious of a speaker's tone of voice, rising inflection, gesture for emphasis or transition of thought.

Campbell was molded by his home, by his educational experiences, by his wide travel opportunities and by the thousands of sermons he heard as well as by the volumes of sermon-books he had read. He had listened to such greats as John Walker, Alexander Carson, Alexander Haldane, and Rowland Hill. He had read such masters as Robert Hall and Robert Blair. He also had put his hand to writing—not sermons—but essays and articles that affected his way of choosing words, forming sentences and organizing ideas.

D. S. Burnet wrote of Campbell, "A scholarly gentleman of another church once said to me he is certainly orthodox in letters whatever may be said of his theology."[4]

In the university Campbell had written essays on a number of themes. Upon arriving in America he soon set out to contribute articles to the Washington (Pennsylvania) *Reporter* under the pen name *Bonus Homo.* When he became a religious editor, he was prolific. What he wrote, though not sermons, became material for the messages delivered Sunday after Sunday by leaders in the churches of Christ being established across the Western Reserve. The magazine itself was considered a "monthly missionary," "a printed preacher," a "Herald of truth" to aid in the "teaching and preaching of Christ."[5] Such constant writing, plus editing the writing of others, kept Campbell precise, vivid, and accurate, while he chose to speak extemporaneously rather than to read a manuscript. Others might "in a single discourse break the whole ten commandments of the King's English."[6] Campbell would honor the gospel by clothing it in the fitting attire of fine grammar.

Where many at that time who were affected by the Great Revival could not in their enthusiasm wait for a thorough preparation for the ministry, Campbell underwent a broad education. As the uneducated clergy among such as the Baptists could not hide that omission, Campbell's sermons could not conceal his learning. When he debated he could draw to his side standard, scholarly works. When he conversed with literary or scientific men in the drawing room, he was at home in their terminology. When he delivered a lecture by request upon language, the state, philosophy, education or other themes,[7] the reporters pronounced him a complete master of his subject and the audiences agreed that they had listened to the thinking of a great mind. When he preached, he seemed to draw without effort from the rich fund of interesting matter stored in his mind. Each sermon confirmed the fact that beyond his formal education of sixteen years, he on many days had spent sixteen hours[8] in his library.

VIII LIFE AND LABORS
Campbell's Ministry

Campbell once said that the Bible, being a book of history, should be studied through the two eyes of chronology and geography. The same historical consciousness should be applied in a survey of the times and places in Campbell's history that are landmarks in his preaching career.

The place of his birth was Ireland—more specifically, county Antrim, the community was Ballymena, and the house was the Presbyterian manse. The time of his birth was September 12, 1788. In 1807, while his father sailed for the new world, Alexander at the age of nineteen was gaining public instruction by filling Thomas' shoes as teacher at Rice Hill (Ireland).

When the Campbell family attempted to follow Thomas to America by setting sail on October 1, 1808, they were shipwrecked six days later in the Hebrides on the isle of Islay. Though at an early date Thomas had planted the idea of becoming a preacher in Alexander's mind, this providential rescue of the family was a major factor in the son's final decision "to spend his entire life in the ministry of the gospel."[1]

This diversion from the proposed direct route to America placed Campbell in Glasgow by November 3, 1808, allowing him for a year to become a student under the formative influence of the University. A month after arriving in America he was in Washington, (western) Pennsylvania reading the "Declaration and Address" written by his father for the Christian Association of that city, a group organized August 17, 1809. His own growing convictions regarding the sin of church division, were catalyzed by this document of his father and he devoted the rest of his life to the promotion of Christian unity.

Where youthfulness and lack of experience had earlier kept him from taking public part in the worship services his father conducted, at the parent's insistence the son, now twenty-two, brought an exhortation at the end of his father's message in the home of Jacob Donaldson. This was so well received that he was asked to preach his first sermon, little suspecting he would preach one hundred and five others before a year had passed. Sermon number one was given before his father's Brush Run congregation on July 15, 1810 in a grove on the farm of Major Templeton, eight miles southwest of Washington. His text for the day was Matthew 7:24-27, and his theme was the comparisons and contrasts of wise and foolish men. The congregation liked it even better than they had liked the preaching of their beloved pastor Thomas Campbell. The Pittsburgh Presbyterian Synod, however, did not appreciate the fact that an unordained man had been allowed to preach. It was not until New Year's Day in 1812 that Campbell was ordained. He was licensed to preach on May 4, 1811 at the time when the Christian Association became an independent church to be governed by the New Testament alone. On that occasion Campbell preached on John 6:48, expounding on the Lord's Supper.

The year 1811 was significant. Campbell had married Margaret Brown (March 12), had moved in with his father-in-law (March 25), had been licensed (May 4), had initiated weekly communion under a towering oak for some sixty or seventy who had been formerly of various denominations (June 16), and had seen his father (himself safely out of the water and perched on a tree root) immerse three of the Brush Run congregation on the fourth of July. He also set out that year on his first of a lifetime of preaching tours. This one was into northeastern Ohio.

After much study regarding the scriptural teaching on ordination, Campbell submitted to the laying on of hands of the local Brush Run Church to become one of their bishops January 1, 1812. Feeling that the same commitment to return to Bible ways forced him to face the question of baptism, he joined his parents and others in immersion at the hands of Elder Mathias Luce at the deep pool in Buffalo Creek. The Brush Run church, now consisting of immersed believers, was received into the Redstone Association of (Regular) Baptist churches.

That Campbell and his congregation were not ever really Baptist became evident as time went on. The cry of heresy ("Antinomianism") went up occasionally before and often after his famous "Sermon on the Law"[2] delivered September 1, 1816 before the Redstone Association convened at Cross Creek, Brooke County, Virginia. During the sermon a lady fainted; Elder Pritchard, recognizing that it was not Baptist doctrine, called out some of the preachers (Estep, Wheeler and others); and the decision was made to bring the message to trial when the Association came together next at Peter's Creek in 1817. Perhaps the reformation Campbell advocated would never have been proclaimed so energetically had it not been for the opposition begun here.

The point of the message was that while the Old Testament law was temporary and local, the New Testament gospel was for all time and universal. Campbell viewed revelation as progressive as he traced it through the Patriarchal, Jewish and Christian dispensations and he termed these "starlight, moonlight and sunlight." John the Baptist was the "twilight" preceding the full blaze of revelation coming in Christ. As Christ was superior to Moses, the gospel was superior to the law. According to the Preface written thirty years after the sermon, present popular Christianity was considered "a compound of Judaism, heathen philosophy and Christianity; which like the materials in Nebuchadnezzar's image, does not cement together."[3]

While this sermon was called for just two hours before delivery, upon the sudden illness of the scheduled speaker, the idea had been in his thoughts for at least four years as the recently found records of his early sermons confirm.[4]

Wherever Campbell went people were curious to hear his views and were anxious to listen to his able defense of the plea for unity in Christ alone. Before the "Sermon on the Law" a few in Philadelphia, New York and Washington, D. C. heard him in a tour to the East during 1815, soliciting funds for a Wellsburg meeting-house. After that sermon, the spreading word—both pro and con—added to his attendants. In 1817 he advocated the new plea throughout Western Pennsylvania, West Virginia and Eastern Ohio. To further assist the reform he opened the Buffalo Seminary in 1818 (Bethany College in 1840), entered the arena of debate with John Walker in 1820 (with McCalla in 1823, Owen in 1829, Purcell in 1837, and Rice in 1843) and began the *Christian Baptist* in 1823 (the *Millennial Harbinger* in 1830).

The preaching tours were second to none as influence for the reformation. His thinking was spread throughout the Union, especially the "3,000,000 acres of nine counties which constituted the Western Reserve," into Canada and across the sea to Britain, Scotland and Ireland. The time was ripe. America was expanding across the continent; the political and economic systems were promising a whole new way of life; and the population was burgeoning, growing in the United States from nearly thirteen million in 1830 to over twenty-four million in 1850. Freedom and independence were in the air. Men were talking at lyceums, literary societies, college lectureships and learned associations of all kinds; audiences were ready to listen to any speech, and especially to such a clear and simple, lucid and learned presentation as Campbell could make.

Campbell was a liberal calling for improvement without loss of past values. He advocated emancipation of slaves yet free of anarchy, catholicism free of Romanism, protestantism free from sectarianism, biblical truth free from opinionism, fundamental faith free from creedalism, and reformation free from all fear of failure. Every fly-leaf of every issue of the *Millennial Harbinger* carried the quotation: "Great is the truth and mighty above all things, and will prevail!" Campbell's undergirding assurance was that while skeptics could doubt and guilty men could fear, those who trust God's promises could only know victory.

The *Millennial Harbinger* contained the planned itinerary prior to a journey to encourage a hearing; and following the fact reports of the results and the messages were given in the periodical. The articles were titled "Notes on a Tour to New York, via Eastern Virginia;" "Sketch of a Tour of Seventy-Five Days;" "Of Sixteen Hundred Miles;" "Notes on a Tour to the North-East" (this included eleven states); "Incidents on a Tour to the South;" "To Eastern Cities;" "To the West;" "To the Far West;" "To the South-West;" "To Canada West;" "Letters from Europe;" "My Imprisonment in Glasgow;" "Our Excursion through Ohio;" "To Iowa;" "To Baltimore and Washington City;" "To Illinois;" "To Nashville;" "To Pittsburgh and Allegheny Cities;" "To Southern Kentucky;" *etc.*. Local papers in the various communities and religious journals of the various denominations likewise announced his coming and reacted to his sermons.

The addresses disseminated his principles of reform; and often increased the contributions to his college. The debates did more to secure followers than a year of preaching. The lectures on topics not strictly religious[5] broadened numerically his audiences and increased his reputation significantly. The convention speeches to his own followers deepened their admiration and stirred their ardor. The baccalaureate addresses each fourth of July at Bethany College by its president were as expected and desired as were his morning lectures each school-day throughout the years.

Articles on Campbell often speak of his robust health and his freedom from illness until the very final days of his life. The tour records, however, show Campbell to have been troubled by a common preacher problem—fatigue and hoarseness. Damp and cold weather, or overuse of the voice in public and private gatherings, obliged him to miss some appointments or to call for medical assistance. He had his own quaint way of tackling the problem, as revealed in this incident:

I had contracted so severe a cold in journeying in the bleak, moist winds of that week, that on my arrival in Independence, my voice was completely taken away, so as not to be able to articulate or clearly enunciate a single sentence . . . By the philosophy of a sound sleep, after a two hour's bath in a wet sheet, my voice was restored so that I was enabled, next day, to deliver a discourse.[6]

The aging Alexander Campbell, who attended his last general convention in 1864 and submitted his last article for the *Millennial Harbinger* in 1865, preached his last sermon in 1866. The topic was "the spiritual blessings in heavenly places in Christ" from Ephesians, chapter one. The presentation was as vigorous as in the early days; however, about six weeks later when he (now seventy-eight years of age and weakened from many days of confinement) set out to speak, his son-in-law, W. K. Pendleton, noting his weakness, encouraged him to give way to Robert Richardson. On the Lord's Day, which was March 4, 1866, at fifteen minutes before it turned into Monday, Alexander Campbell expired. Richardson records that occasionally during his final years, Campbell's wife would be awakened by his preaching during sleep. The theme one night very shortly before his passing was Christ's second coming.[7]

IX SOURCES AND STRUCTURE
Campbell's Sermons

When we examine Campbell's hymn-book,[1] prepared for the worshipping church, it is possible to say that Christ and Christ alone was his theme. That hymnal had three sections —Psalms, Hymns and Spiritual Songs. The Psalms were songs on the life of Christ arranged in chronological order. The Hymns, each following the example of the Book of Revelation, were addressed in praise to Christ as the Lamb upon the throne. The Spiritual Songs, while upon other biblical themes, were placed in the hymnal to enable the Christians to "teach one another (Col. 3:16) all that Christ "had commanded" (Matt. 28:19).

Looking into Campbell's sermon notes, as in his hymnal, it is equally valid to speak of Christ as Campbell's all-absorbing theme. He clearly was a preacher of the Bible, especially of the New Testament, and most especially of Christ. In sampling the texts referred to either in Campbell's original sermon notes, or in records concerning where and what he preached, we find that of one hundred forty-six messages tested only sixteen had Old Testament passages as their basic texts (however, even here according to his custom he drew illustrations for his theme from the entire range of biblical history). When he did choose a passage of Old Testament Scripture, it was a New Testament truth that he illumined: such as the Lord's Supper from the Song of Solomon,[2] the progressive light of revelation from Genesis 1:3[3] or the New Testament Church from the typology of the Old Testament Tabernacle.[4] The entire Bible from Moses the lawgiver to John the revelator had Christ as its single theme.

Upon taking a text from the gospels, epistles or apocalypse, the announced subject might be prayer, covenants or edification, but the actual theme was Christ the intercessor in prayer, Jesus the mediator of the New Covenant, or the living Word the all-sufficient theme of the church.

Christ's person, Christ's work, Christ's character, Christ's perfection, Christ's supremacy, Christ's glory, Christ's revelation, Christ's salvation, Christ's life, death, burial, resurrection, ascension and glorification were the topics of Scripture and the message of Campbell. Having the single theme of Christ for preaching and teaching did not lead to monotony. The list of Campbell's first year of preaching shows sixty-one varied topics in the one hundred and six messages.[5] A series of lectures in Nottingham thirty-seven years later indicates similar unity in variety. The five subjects were: "Has God ever spoken to man? The Kingdom of Heaven. The Holy Spirit. The Gospel of Jesus Christ, and the Principles of Christian Union."[6] Enough scattered material on these subjects is found in Campbellian sources to show that Christ was the basic subject of each message no matter how varied were the announced topics.

If the reoccurence of certain themes and texts in the notes of a preaching tour, does not imply the reuse of the very same sermon, it at least suggests that some subjects and biblical passages had become favorites of Campbell. Mrs. Campbell said that while her husband often spoke on the same topics, such themes were sufficiently "varied and enlarged" to be always fresh and absorbing.[7] A contributor to the *Millennial Harbinger*, signing only the initials "J. W." agreed:

> We had the privilege of hearing brother Campbell on the same topic when in Banbury and Newcastle . . . Not, indeed, that it could be the same discourse. No: this would be impossible; for no two, even on the same topic are alike. The different points investigated—the illustrations so varied, *etc*.[8]

Among the early records Campbell made of his preaching engagements is one chart divided into sixty-six sections for the sixty-six books of his canon of Scripture.[9] Under each biblical book he had listed all the sermons he had preached to that date from some passage in that particular section of Scripture. This appears to indicate an early desire on his part not to neglect any portion of the inspired writings in his pulpit ministry. Campbell decided later on that the better way to give a congregation the thorough view of Scripture was not to select a text from each book over a long period of time, but to give scope and dimension to every sermon by setting each passage in its broadest context and by drawing illustrations from the vast expanse of biblical history.

From 1 Timothy 3:16 Campbell preached "On the Justification and Coronation of the Messiah." This sermon was written in full for publication in Kentucky during 1850 and was included with messages by twenty-seven religious leaders from various denominational bodies. It is copied in his wife's work on his *Home Life*. Matthew 28:18-20 and Mark 16:15, 16 were often the passages used on a missionary occasion. Hebrews 1 offered thoughts on God's last message by his son and Hebrews 11 on the faith that saves. The good confession in Matthew 16:16-18 was many times proclaimed as the only foundation of Christian union, communion and co-operation that is "broad enough, or strong enough to sustain Christ's own church of all nations and of all ages."[10] Another unity text was John 17 or Ephesians 4:4-6. Each case of conversion in the Book of Acts was foundation for a message with apostolic authority on how men are saved. Man's salvation and the church's unity were Campbell's major concerns. He held no doubt that his co-laborers "had got hold of the great principles of ecclesiastical union and communion on which all real Christians of all denominations, might, could and certainly *would* one day unite."[11]

In order to give a local congregation the whole counsel of God, he covered the moral and religious field with a lesson on marriage, another on fasting, still others on predestination, judgment, apostasy, conscience, justification, mediation, and spiritual gifts, to name a few. All of these subjects and more were discussed in the light of the apostle's doctrine.

When Campbell announced his topic and text, the congregation at that point still did not know how he would develop it. In Lexington, Campbell, taking Christ's interview with Nicodemus for a text, compared the three kingdoms of nature, grace and glory. He showed each: (1) to be created by a word of God, (2) designed to produce natural, gracious and glorious beings, (3) proposed to live natural, spiritual and eternal lives, (4) introduced by natural, gracious and glorious births, (5) from the flesh, from water and the Spirit, and from the grave, (6) enjoying a salvation from natural danger, from the guilt, pollution and power of sin over the soul, and of the body from the grave.[12] The conclusion stressed the impossibility of being in any of the three kingdoms without a birth into it. According to all available reports, Campbell's sermon on 1 Corinthians 13 was especially impressive dealing with Christian faith, hope and love as it showed the first to be founded on the witnessed facts concerning Christ, the second on the promises given by Christ, and "the greatest" of all on the beautiful holiness and character of Christ.

Since Revelation 14:6-7 was quoted on every flyleaf of the *Millennial Harbinger* when he topically dealt with the "everlasting gospel" of this passage, Campbell reasoned that the term "everlasting" was fitting as applied to the "gospel" because of its eternal author, abiding covenant, lasting foundation and continuing effects (everlasting righteousness, salvation, consolation, victory and glory).[13]

Sometimes the major points of an outline were put in the form of questions that people ask: "What am I? Whence came I? Whither do I go?"[14] What is the whole world? Does its gain necessarily imply the loss of the soul? Is not that life great that could gain all the world? What is presupposed in the "so" loving the world that the soul is lost.[15] His Sermon on the Law was an effort to answer the questions: what "the law" means, what it could not accomplish, why it failed and how God remedied its defects. A popular lecture often given to college students or skeptical audiences raised and answered four questions: Has God ever spoken to man? In what language has he spoken? If in human language, how is it to be interpreted? and What has he said to us in his last message by his Son?[16] An early communion sermon asked what we were to do, how, why, how often and with what consequences and advantages.[17]

At other times, in the place of proposed questions, the outline was one of chronological consciousness: "Christianity as it was, as it is, and as it ought to be;"[18] or Christ's kingdom in origin, progress and ultimate triumph; or, again, the great leaders of men: Moses, John and Jesus (their attestations, their promises and threatenings, and the place of passing through water on the part of their disciples—the immersion into Moses in cloud and sea, into reformation at the Jordan, and into the name of the Father, Son and Holy Spirit in Christian baptism).[19]

The major points of the outline many times were numerous, such as when he spoke of the kingdom of Christ in its constitution, government, subjects, laws, privileges and marks;[20] or when he taught concerning the judgment under Christ relating to its preparation, judge, person's judged, manner and the trial's subject.[21]

In those instances that the basic organization was simple, the subpoints were often extensive. For example, when he spoke on ordination among Jews, Christians and that relating to the pastoral office, he used nine examples in the first division, five in the second and four in the third.[22] In a two-point message on hidden and revealed things, to the first item he asks what the hidden things are, from whom they are hidden and in what manner they are hidden. On the second topic he again asks to whom, in what manner and why some items are revealed.[23]

When he spoke on the doctrine of baptism "by special request," he expounded its action, its legitimate subject and its design, taking time during the last division to refute the allegation that "Campbellites" gave the virtue of Christ's blood to baptismal water. This he denied, reasoning that his opponents "might as truthfully charge upon us the doctrine of Roman Transubstantiation, because we quote the words 'this is my body,' 'this is my blood,' in dispensing the monumental loaf and cup."[24] On a trip to Tennessee Campbell preached on the "Seven Baptisms" that exist when you go beyond the "one baptism" extant when Paul addressed the Ephesians. He dealt with infant baptism, Quaker baptism, John's baptism, fire baptism, Holy Spirit baptism, metaphorical baptism and "the one immersion, or Christian baptism."[25]

Viewing the ordinance of the Lord's Supper from the vantage point of 1 Corinthians 11:23-29, he looked at its commemorative intention, its symbolic nature, its practical use and its necessary qualifications on the part of a worshipper.[26] At another time on the same passage he illustrated how the gospel is preached in words, in ordinances and in the lives of its professors.[27]

> Religion, my Christian brethren, as the term indicates, began after the Fall. Holy men and angels did not need faith, repentance, prayer, altars, priests, victims, rites, or religious usages, to bring them back, or bind them fast to God. The word *religion*, indeed, imparts a previous apostasy.[28]

So began a sermon on prayer that stressed four indispensables to successful prayer: a mediator, faith, repentance and the teachings of the Holy Spirit. "We preach the gospel when we say be damned as well as when we say be saved,"[29] was the opening sentence of a message from Mark 16:16 regarding the faith that saves. At another time the same apostolic commission to preach to every creature was read, with this statement its immediate follow-up: "Wide as humanity and enduring as time, or till every son of Adam hears the message of salvation, extends this commission in its letter, spirit, and obligation."[30] To initiate the teaching on progressive revelation, Campbell simply read a line from Genesis 1:3 and immediately added one pithy, thought-challenging sentence: "'God said, Let there be light, and light was.' This was the first speech ever made within our universe."[31]

To capture attention, as he launched into the sermon preparing for the first celebration of the Lord's Supper at Brush Run, Campbell having read the Scripture John 6:48, 58 said: "Sin, death, and misery entered the world by eating. So may righteousness, life and joy come to us."[32]

A study of Campbell's sermon introductions seems to indicate that they were intended to gain the attention of the audience and then to interest it in the subject he intended to treat. Judge Jeremiah Sullivan Black, Chief Justice of Pennsylvania and later Attorney General of the United States, said that "the first sentence of his discourse 'drew the audience still as death.'"[33] This was likely the case in Scotland when the Paisley Baptist congregation, in expectancy to hear a man for the first time whose reputation was that of an undramatic speaker that opposed text-preaching, saw Campbell enter the pulpit, look around for a moment, lift the open Bible in his hands, and begin: "We are not in the habit of taking a verse out of a chapter, or a clause out of a verse, for a text to preach from. We take the Bible, the whole Bible, and nothing but the Bible, for a text, and preach from it." Setting the Bible down on the pulpit, he continued: "On this occasion, we shall depart from our usual practice, and take the thirteenth chapter of first Corinthians and thirteenth verse."[34]

The introductions were not long for a sermon that might last two to six times as long as those preached by his successors. The conclusions were also comparatively brief, but also intensely practical. If non-Christians were addressed, and they were deemed ready for harvesting the "necessity of immediate submission"[35] to Christ was enforced and the hearers left in no doubt regarding the definite things God was asking them to do. They were not to tarry, or pray, but to obey the gospel commands of repentance and baptism. They could declare their faith by standing where they were and openly avowing Christ. The body of the sermon was an appeal to the understanding to produce faith; the conclusion permitted an appeal to the heart or feelings to act on what they now believed.

When the hearers were Christians gathered for edification, they were to see the practical application of all that was said and to be exhorted by specific appeals to live the life of a Christian. To conclude an address to a mixed audience ("mongrel races of modern times, part Jews, and part

Christians") was more difficult than any effort by the apostles. "To convert such a people from error to truth—from theory to practice—from disobedience to obedience—from Satan to Christ—*this* is the work that requires the wisdom of a Paul and the eloquence of an Apollos."[36]

The illustration books on which Campbell relied for analogies were three—the Bible, the book of nature, and history. If the audience followed agricultural pursuits, several illustrations might be used well-suited to their understanding. If they were Bible students, appeal could be made to the events of both Testaments. If they knew history, its happenings were illustrative of biblical principles. Christ and his apostles had drawn from these same sources in illustrating their teachings. Campbell's broad education, extensive travels, wide experiences and keen memory provided readily proverbs, poetry, maxims, quotations and facts.

He used chaste, homely, vivid and apt analogies, and never told a string of anecdotes to appeal to the ears itching for fine illustrations. He would never string out a series of death-bed stories. Any story was to bring clarity to the truth enunciated and neither to embellish nor call attention to itself. For this reason "those who looked for pepper and salt and vinegar were surprised to receive manna, wine and oil."[37]

As Campbell stated his proposition, proved and illustrated it, he would regularly summarize and restate to keep the listeners clear as to his main point. All the subpoints and illustrations contributed directly to the conclusion he had in mind. Often the audience was informed from the beginning exactly where the sermon would lead. At other times he would move from one seemingly unconnected point to another, until at length perception would come almost at once regarding their necessary relationship. Richardson observed, it is "as some Napoleon directs at various distant points large and isolated bodies of troops, whose destination cannot be determined by ordinary minds until the unexpected concentration of the whole upon a given point reveals the comprehensive genius of the warrior."[38]

Like a warrior, Campbell set upon preaching the sermon with a definite plan based upon his analysis of the audience and the theme. Did not his preaching examples, the inspired apostles, contemplate the men before them "as believers or as unbelievers—as practicing or not practicing the precepts of the Savior" and then immediately propose some point "in reference to which they opened the scriptures and applied them?"[39] Had not Campbell himself advised young preachers to "first of all ascertain the stature of the mind, or the amount of information which his audience may be supposed to possess"[40] as the foundation upon which they would build?

To make an audience wiser in the ways of the Lord required disciplined study on the part of the teacher or preacher. A spokesman's ambition ought to be becoming "mighty in the Scriptures" rather than "accomplished scholars or mighty in human learning."[41] To be able to teach others the Bible in its proper contextual connection or the scriptural testimony on a given topic (and in either case speaker and hearer grapple directly with the Bible itself), preachers must know clearly what they are going to show others. Since Campbell saw that it required hours of study in many instances "to read one verse or chapter in the Bible, so as to produce the proper effect,"[42] he spent many hours daily in his library. There among carefully selected books, he spent most of his time with the one book that contained the message he was to teach. In replying to Robert B. Semple in 1830, Campbell lists the many books he had devoured on a given theme and the many texts he had marshalled in support of the doctrine, but then laments:

I am conscious that I did not understand the New Testament—not a single book of it. Matthew Henry and Thomas Scott were my favorite Commentators. I read the whole of Thomas Scott's Commentary in family worship, section by section. I began to read the scriptures critically. Works of criticism, from Michaelis down to Shark, on the Greek article, were resorted to. While these threw light on many passages, still the book as a whole, the religion of Jesus Christ as a whole was hid from me. I took the *naked text* and followed common sense; it became to me a new book.[43]

Long before breakfast, according to his wife, or reclining in a chair awaiting some meal, according to his biographer, Campbell was reading his Bible according to common-sense rules of interpretation—the usual principles applied to any other writing. That he successfully taught the Scriptures in their context was the conclusion of men like ex-president Madison who considered Campbell "the ablest and most original expounder of the Scripture"[44] he had ever heard.

Scope and dimension are words that define a Campbellian sermon in contrast to what he considered scrap preaching. To pick a phrase from the Bible to meet the needs of the varied audience was "like buying a lottery ticket . . . in the hope of really interesting, and substantially and eternally benefitting, half a dozen of persons." His verdict regarding that type of preaching was that there "are a thousand blanks to one prize!"[45] Each of Campbell's sermons had a wholeness, and while having a text, that passage was placed like a jewel in the setting of the plan of God for man.

X IMPACT AND IMPRESSIONS
Campbell's Influence

Alexander Campbell, who would consider himself but one of the bishops of the Brush Run congregation, was thought of by others as approximating either a messiah or an anti-Christ. The exalted words of praise by his friends regarding his preaching almost causes the reader to blush. The derogatory remarks of his enemies go to the other extreme. Had a Gallup Poll been conducted to determine the favorable or unfavorable impact and impression of Campbell's pulpit achievements, it appears that the results would indicate a landslide in his favor.

A Flemingsburgh, Kentucky clergyman charged Campbell with being a pleaser of men, that is, "the Arian, infidel, horse-racer, and gambler." Yet, he added, "I never heard Campbell preach—I never wish to hear him; but I am convinced he is no gospel preacher."[1] A religious journal, *Watchman of the Prairies*, editorialized concerning him:

> More distinguished for his oratory, wit, and talent, than for his piety, he very soon acquired considerable celebrity, as a public speaker . . . Few persons have ever possessed more of the qualities of a religious demagogue than Alexander Campbell. Eloquent in speech, adroit in argument, witty, ambitious, unscrupulous, and fond of public notoriety, he succeeded, under the most favorable circumstance, in acquiring a popularity

which has given him considerable influence over the minds of many.[2]
From the Columbian Star editor, who wrote, "I never saw Mr. Campbell, but I have been informed,"[3] to the editor of the *Connecticut Journal*, who listed as Campbell's beliefs, what Campbell denied were his beliefs, an expected opposition was manifest by church leaders who disliked his challenge of the *status quo*.

Those who considered themselves delivered from creedal bondage or allegorical interpretations were not hesitant with their expression of admiration. Jeremiah Vardeman declared that "if all the Baptist preachers in Kentucky were put into one, they would not make an Alexander Campbell!"[4] John R. Howard wrote from Illinois to the *Christian Standard* saying, "we regard him as decidedly the greatest man, take him every way, the world has produced since the days of the Apostles."[5] An array of compliments to Campbell's preaching from famous contemporaries can be read by those interested. These may be found in Archibald McLean's small volume *Alexander Campbell as a Preacher* or the chapter "Prince of Preachers" by J. W. Grafton in his book *Alexander Campbell Leader of the Great Reformation of the Nineteenth Century*.[6] These authors did not omit the encomiums on Campbell as did the correspondent of an English periodical, the *Bible Advocate*, who felt that what he heard "however merited, did sound *too* exuberant for publication."[7]

What most impressed one admirer was Campbell's grand conceptions, striking illustrations and comprehensive scope.[8] Another was awed by the "freshness of his thought."[9] Still another spoke of "clarity,"[10] "simplicity"[11] or new insights.[12] Most were struck by the conviction of Aylet Rains that Campbell had "more Bible knowledge than any man living."[13] This had been Racoon John Smith's reaction from the first message he had heard, claiming "[Campbell] has thrown more light on the Epistle and on the whole Scriptures, than I have received in all the sermons that I have ever heard before."[14]

We might expect a more objective report on Campbell's impact if we turn from strongly emotioned supporters or foes to the intellectual leaders at a university, the respected editors of major denominational journals and the community's professional men. President Robert Graham of Kentucky University conceived of Campbell as having few equals and no superiors in the pulpit.[15] President Heman Humphrey of Amherst College looked upon him as the most perfectly self-possessed, the most perfectly at ease in the pulpit of any preacher he had listened to.[16] Yale's professor of Theology, Dr. Leonard Bacon, believed him to have "but few, if any, equals among the religious leaders of his time."[17] Where Campbell went to speak to University audiences, if they were not at first struck by his voice, appearance or delivery; the students, like Joseph Brady at Miami University pronounced the speech "the best" they had heard.[18]

An impressive host of names can be displayed, as McLean has done, of editors[19] and historians,[20] doctors[21] and lawyers,[22] and military[23] and national leaders[24] that speak tribute to Campbell as a speaker and preacher. Baptist,[25] Episcopal,[26] Methodist,[27] Presbyterian,[28] Catholic[29] and even sceptical[30] supporters of his eminence in the pulpit can be found with little difficulty. When we read the glowing descriptions of Campbell's method of delivery or subject matter, are we reading the eulogy of a now-dead style of preaching or the words of spectators who have gazed in admiration upon a fresh way of sermon-delivery newly born?

Advocates of Christian unity through a return to apostolic faith and practice not only began to say *what* Alexander

Campbell was saying but attempted to pattern after their ideal in his *way* of speaking. There grew up in Ohio the "School of the Preachers"[31] to mold more adequately the faithful who labored in teaching. At the annual meeting of the churches in that section, the preachers suggested having stated meeting times to improve their skills in the manner of public instruction as well as the matter they presented. Campbell believed the practice of self-criticism would have better fruit than the certain congregational criticism that otherwise would be whispered to the proclaimer's certain disadvantage. At that time there was no other training offered to the spokesmen of the church. By having quarterly gatherings[32] of located and itinerant preachers for mutual correction the gap hopefully could be bridged. For a week of time at a specified place each participant could bring an hour sermon on an assigned theme. This was to be critically examined by his fellow-preachers. The public was welcomed to hear the three or four sermons presented each day but not the thorough review of the messages which included even word pronunciation. The youngest were first asked for comments and finally the oldest. Campbell, who often tried to be present, reported the spirit of the brethren to have been the best and the criticism to have been severe, impartial and beneficial. The first gathering of this kind was the Ohio Western Reserve School at New Lisbon, Saturday to Thursday, December 5 through 10, 1835, when all the speakers dealt with the theme of "principles and rules of interpretation."

The value of these gatherings was immeasurable, since a defect that otherwise might have become an imbedded habit could by the aid of faithful monitors be healed for the benefit of both preacher and hearer. Since not only sermonic matter, form and delivery were discussed but doctrinal questions were raised and debated, these "meetings were not appreciated too highly, as the sequel developed, inasmuch as they disabused the minds of the Baptist ministry in the Mahoning Association of much prejudice and prepared the way for a very great change of views and practice."[33]

Campbell's mark began to show in the preachers under his influence, but did it continue long and does it still remain to this day? While there are entrenched differences in the twentieth century groupings of the "Christian Church (Disciples of Christ)," "Christian Churches" and "Churches of Christ" that all claim rootage in the nineteenth-century reformation, there is a decided similarity in the sermons preached. As William B. Blakemore, Jr. noted in an article for *The Christian Evangelist*,[34] the late "conservative" P. H. Welshimer and the late "liberal" Edward Scribner Ames both preached in Campbellian style. Each approached the Scripture with historic consciousness, each avoided sentimentalism and emotionalism, each revealed well-systematized thought, and each moved from establishing propositions to calling for action based on conviction.

Today, while there are variations within each of these popular groupings, we may observe that in some areas the present-day Christian Church (Disciples of Christ) appears to be moving from Campbell in the realm of preaching. Some among this denomination would tend to see more social implications in the four Gospels than he saw and would consider preaching social concerns the legitimate and necessary work of today's pulpit.[35] Some among them would "not readily agree that its [the New Testament's] specific admonitions are to be specifically obeyed as the voice of God," or that they should consider themselves "reformers" rather than "churchmen," or that they should "launch out without regard to the past in the same way that Campbell did."[36] If Campbell were to return he might wonder if the eldership had not surrendered its teaching responsibility,

111

and he would question the garb the preachers wore, the clerical position they assumed and the titles by which they were called.

Christians from "independent" Christian Churches in this day assemble at such gatherings as the North American Christian Convention which is known as a "preaching" convention in contrast to a business convention. While many of the messages they hear have Campbellian traits, there occasionally is revealed a use of anecdote, jest, or manuscript reading not in harmony with Campbell's opinions regarding teaching. These speakers are usually schooled in Bible Colleges rather than in Liberal Arts schools where the Bible is the central text. The preachers possibly have given more attention to oratorical skills than Campbell thought wise and occasionally have used texts in a way reminiscent of the "scrap preaching" or "proof-texting" to which Campbell objected. If Campbell dropped in to such a convention he would doubtless ask where were the elite minds, the visiting denominational clergy or the interested skeptics that used to be found in his meetings. Most of all he might be inquisitive to know why a Bible people did not find it helpful to hear preaching with the Bible open before each hearer.

Even among the most conservative of all these segments that look back to Campbell, the Churches of Christ have some congregations where a clergyman exists in fact while denied in theory. On a Sunday morning when Christians are gathered to remember the Christ who purchased their salvation, they are apt to hear a sermon "preached" to them as if they were the world in need of conversion rather than the saints in need of edification that comes through teaching. By asking around it might be learned that the members had not studied the Scriptures at home in preparation for the discourse. By looking around it might be noted that the speaker is not concluding his message with dialogue nor addressing (even at a Christian college lectureship) the inclusive crowd of sectarian Christians that Campbell hoped to reach with his principles of reform.

By these random examples we are attempting to suggest that in those religious bodies where Campbell's name is still heard, there is some evidence of his impact still abiding, but at the same time there is a clear indication that certain of his insights are being lost, forgotten or rejected.

The articles he wrote on preaching are not easily available but are to be found only in a few libraries. The sermons he preached have, but for a few exceptions, been unrecorded for posterity. It is time for every "Christian only," as well as every preacher and teacher among them, to ask afresh: Are the principles of union and reform he proposed valid? Does the church today want or need preaching as he conceived it? Where is there in all the millions who count themselves members of the Christian Church (Disciples of Christ), Christian Churches or Churches of Christ one modern voice that holds sway among the masses and the intellectuals as did the voice of Alexander Campbell?

It is a temptation at this point to scathe with words those groups which in my opinion are falling short of the high heritage passed on by Alexander Campbell. Three considerations keep me from yielding to the compulsion. Many individual teachers and preachers refuse to fit into oversimplified catagories. The Bible does raise this issue: "Who are you to pass judgment on the servant of another? It is before his own master that he stands or falls" (Rom. 14:4, R.S.V.). And to offend a reader will bring no reformation, but to invite all who preach the gospel to join in testing their understanding and practice by the insights of Campbell will result in renewal wherever it is sought.

Campbell was convinced that all church reformation would need to begin with those who took the position of preachers and teachers of the Word. In expounding the faith, hope, and love of Paul's 1 Corinthians 13:13, Campbell wrote: "A reformation in pulpit oratory must antedate any true or real reformation in the church going community, as respects its edification and piety."[37] Those words have profound relevance and suggestive guidance for all who desire Christians to be one in Christ so that the world can be won to Christ. If Alexander Campbell was right in his claim that the shortest route to a unity that is lasting and Christian is a return to the faith and practice of apostolic times, it is imperative that preachers and teachers of Christ reform their preaching by New Testament standards and become preachers of reform bringing renewal to the church and the world.

XI CONCLUDING OBSERVATIONS

We have been viewing the life of a man who held some distinctive ideas about preaching and who used preaching as a means of creating the Christian fellowship he had read about in the New Testament Scriptures. Neither the revivalistic preaching that abandoned reason nor the denominational proclamation of party opinion was the need of the hour. The world would never be informed of God's wondrous plan for its salvation by messengers that took the scrap of a text out of its context and shouted for an hour on their experiences or strung out anecdotes about the experiences of others. In the preaching described in the New Testament, proclaiming the news about Christ, with accompanying promises, commands and warnings was quite otherwise; but for serious churchmen it ought to be accepted as normative.

Bible Christians would soon find the Holy Spirit had used in the written Word of God precise words to define the work of specified functionaries. Preaching was the evangelist's work to convert the world, establish churches and set things in order. Teaching was the ministry of local church elders so that all new converts having been brought into the school of Christ by baptism might be taught to observe all that Jesus had commanded his followers.

Those who labored as teachers or preachers of Christ in every place throughout Christian history were called by their congregation to that humble ministry because of their observed capabilities. They were not to do all the work but to train all members for their varied ministries. Each such man pressed into the work of the pulpit was not to expect the kind of call an apostle of Christ received; but he was expected to live the kind of life the apostles exemplified— lives of modesty, prayerful earnestness, dignity, purity, and loving wisdom.

The audience a speaker addressed was to be made to think. The spokesman for the church was to bring a message from the mind of God to the mind of man. God had so made man that the faith in Christ which He desired could be produced in man by the evidence He provided in the apostolic witness. Hence, he that would make believers must not waste his time telling of his religious or political opinions, his orthodoxy or heterodoxy; but he must state, establish and illustrate what God had done in Christ. He that would edify believers would wisely limit his terminology to biblical words, while giving biblical scope and dimension in every presentation in a way that is true to the biblical context. The sermons exemplified in the Bible were extemporaneously delivered in a conversational style and had marks of dialogue.

Alexander Campbell tried to be that kind of preacher and teacher one reads about in the New Testament. With the encouragement of a godly wife, the Bible-memorizing habit of inspirational parents and the practice of personal discipline which made Campbell spend sixteen hours a day in his library, he became an expert in one book. Broadening travel, a liberal education and constant writing and editing kept that one book in its proper perspective. His ministry reveals the development of his concepts and the victories won in turning skeptics into Christians and narrow sectarians into catholic-minded Christians.

Campbell's theme was Christ and his basic interests were the church's unity and the world's salvation. His sermon texts were primarily from the New Testament but always illustrated from the wide range of biblical history. To hear him was to fill the mind with truths from history and nature that led to conviction regarding and commitment to the truth.

Some in the nineteenth century thought too highly of Campbell, but all respected him for his Bible knowledge. At that time almost all under his shadow sought to preach as he did. Today, however, while his brand is visible in congregations related to the Restoration Movement, no group in the fellowship could claim to measure up fully to his ideal. Many would not be cognizant of that ideal. Some might not agree with it. Yet, those who rethink preaching in the light of Campbell's observations will be benefited.

Two relevant questions now press us. In the church of tomorrow can any of Campbell's insights be used to make the church come alive? What are the universals that worked for him as a preacher that will work for any gospel proclaimer or church reformer that uses them now?

Renewal, like faith, comes from hearing the Word of God. The reform Campbell preached, like all church reforms before and since, grew out of a serious searching of the Scriptures. The will of God was sought in that source. What is the "gospel?" What is the meaning of the order to "preach" it? How was that gospel communicated by the early church? Such questions call for a wrestling of the modern mind with the ancient texts.

Like both renewal and faith, Christian oneness comes from hearing afresh the Word of God. In the document of Scripture is to be found the unity Christ seeks for his

117

church, the way of its attainment and the creation of that spirit necessary to its manifestation. There must be a norm for the unity of Christians and it must be as old as Christ's apostles. The church must return to faith in and obedience to Christ as the single bond of that unity. The atmosphere conducive to ecumenical attainment must be that of love and freedom. Lasting unity must guarantee the integrity of the individual and grant to him as a believer in the Lordship of Christ the right to think for himself. The free individual and the free congregation spontaneously cooperating out of love for Christ, his will and his people is the unity desired.

The effective preaching method of Campbell that will bear fruit for today's ministers of the Word is based on the rights of the congregation as a school of Christ. An assembly of Christians has the right to expect to hear that which is relevant to their lives. As disciples of Christ they have the right to expect to hear the gospel of Christ and not the discipline of another teacher. As students of the "master teacher" they have the right to expect in the passing of time, with their cooperative effort, to become educated from the pulpit in the subjects of the Scripture. The teachers of the Word are to defend and stimulate the student body to think for itself and to ask questions and share in dialogue on the teachings of Jesus. The preacher or teacher must establish a vital proposition with evidence and logic and by persuasion gain the desired response in life. The extemporaneous style and natural manner of a minister well-educated in history, literary arts and Bible will be productive of good. Great preaching results when, as with Campbell, Christ is the theme, charity the tone, clarity the route and certainty the foundation. In a world of human doubts the church bears the message of divine assurance.

REFERENCES

Table of Abbreviations

CB   *The Christian Baptist*
MH   *The Millenial Harbinger*
MEMOIRS   Robert Richardson, *Memoirs of Alexander Camp-
            bell.* (Cincinnati: Standard Publishing Co., 1897)
            2 vols. Reprinted by The Gospel Advocate Com-
            pany, Nashville, Tenn.

Citations to *The Millennial Harbinger* do not reflect the various series of this periodical. The following table will serve as a bibliographical guide for the interested researcher.

Series I	1830-1836
Series II	1837-1843
Series III	1844-1850
Series IV	1851-1857
Series V	1858-1864

All citations are from material authored by Alexander Campbell unless otherwise noted.

CHAPTER I—New Resources for Campbell Study

[1]"The Christian Missionary Society, no. 1," *MH* 7, no. 2 (February 1850): 75.

[2]"Letters to England, No. VIII," *MH* 2, no. 4 (April 1, 1838): 181.

[3]Selina Huntington Campbell, *Home Life and Reminiscences of A. Campbell by His Wife* (St. Louis: John Burns, 1882), p. 124.

[4]"Editorial Notices," *MH* 1, no. 2 (February, 1851): 113.

[5]"Our New Year's Gift," *MH* 1, no. 2 (February, 1851): 85-96.

[6]For example, "A Discourse Delivered in the Church at Bethany, Va., Oct. 17th, by James M. Macrum, of Pittsburgh," *MH* 2, no. 1 (January 1859): 23ff.; or "Sermons of the Rev. C. H. Spurgeon: The Glorious Habitation," *MH* 6, no. 9 (September, 1863): 385.

[7]*MH* 3, no. 4 (May, 1839): 204-207; *MH* 3, no. 11 (November, 1860): 673ff.

[8](Cincinnati: H. S. Bosworth, 1867) pp. 305ff.

[9]*Discipliana,* November, 1964, p. 62.

[10]*Preaching in the Thought of Alexander Campbell* (St. Louis: The Bethany Press, 1954). Dwight E. Stevenson, Professor of Homiletics at Lexington Theological Seminary, in the 1969 Forrest F. Reed Lectures of the Disciples of Christ Historical Society dealt

ALEXANDER CAMPBELL

with Campbell and others under the general theme, "Disciple Preaching in the First Generation: An Ecological Study."

CHAPTER II—Needs and Norms

[1] *Memoirs,* 1, p. 487.

[2] "Sermons to Young Preachers, No. I," *CB* 7, no. 2 (September 7, 1829): 46. For a description of emotional preaching and its effects at Cane Ridge, Kentucky see John Rogers, *The Biography of Elder Barton Warren Stone* (Cincinnati: J. A. and U. P. James, 1847), pp. 30-64.

[3] "Notes on a Tour to the North-East—No. VI," *MH* 7, no. 10 (October, 1836): 508.

[4] "Address to the Readers of the Christian Baptist," *CB* 1, no. 6 (January 5, 1824): 115.

[5] "The Clergy—No. IV," *CB* 1, no. 6, (January 5, 1824): 108-109.

[6] "The Christian Preacher—No. III," *MH* 3, no. 5 (May 2, 1832): 234.

[7] "Notes on a Tour in Iowa," *MH* 1, no. 1 (January, 1858): 24.

[8] "Practical Thoughts and Reflections," *MH* 5, no. 3 (March, 1848): 146. A contributor to the *Millennial Harbinger* signing himself *Thomas* tells that his preacher in nine years explained to him one hundred eight texts "equal to two chapters in Matthew" (December, 1833), p. 589.

[9] "Review of a Sermon," *CB* 3, no. 8 (March 6, 1826): 156.

[10] A point made by Campbell in a sermon on Matthew 11:27 preached in Brush Run (*Memoirs,* I, p. 375).

[11] "Texts and Textuary Divines," *CB* 2, no. 10 (May 2, 1825): 189.

[12] "A Familiar Dialogue, Between the Editor and a Clergyman, Part I," *CB* 1, no. 12 (June 5, 1824): 234-235.

[13] "Church Edification: an Address delivered before the Kentucky Convention, held at Harrodsburg, Ky. September 28, 1853" *MH* 3, no. 10 (October, 1853): 552.

[14] "Synopsis of Reformation Principles and Objects. Chapter I," *MH* 1, no. 12 (December, 1837): 532-533.

[15] "Practical Thoughts and Reflections," *MH* 4, no. 3 (March, 1847): 153.

[16] "Practical Thoughts and Reflections," *MH* 3, no. 5 (May, 1846): 283; "The Christian Missionary Society—No. I," *MH* 7, no. 2 (February, 1850): 75.

[17] *Memoirs,* I, p. 138.

References

[18]Alexander Campbell, "Humble Beginnings," *MH* 6, no. 1 (January, 1842): 5.

[19]Alexander Campbell, "A Word to the Moral Regenerators of this Age," *MH* 2, no. 6 (August 5, 1833): 380-381.

[20]In a sermon on Matthew 16:13-20 Campbell makes Jesus' manner of teaching the first half of the discourse. See "Notes on a Tour To Eastern Virginia—No. II," *MH* 6, no. 3 (March, 1856): 136-139.

[21]Robert Richardson, "Nature of Christian Doctrine—No. I," *MH* 6, no. 4 (April, 1856):"203, footnote.

[22]"The Christian Preacher—No. V," *MH* 3, no. 7 (July 2, 1832): 306-310; 3, no. 8 (August, 1832): 400-403; 3, no. 9 (September 3, 1832): 467-469; "Letters from Europe—No. XXVIII," *MH* 5, no. 6 (June, 1848): 337; "Notes on a Tour to Eastern Virginia," *MH* 6, no. 2 (February, 1856): 83.

[23]"Letters to England—No. III," *MH* 1, no. 8 (August, 1837): 380.

CHAPTER III—Terms and Tasks

[1]The restoration of pure speech, or the calling of Bible things by Bible names was the first principle "for the healing of divisions amongst Christians and the better understanding of the Christian Institution." See "Synopsis of Reformation Principles and Objects," *MH* 1, no. 12 (December, 1837): 530.

[2]"The Christian Ministry," a discourse by Francis Wayland with comments by Alexander Campbell, *MH* 4, no. 6 (June, 1854): 304.

[3]"Church Edification: An Address delivered before the Kentucky Convention, held at Harrodsburg, Ky. September 28, 1853," *MH* 3, no. 10 (October, 1853): 541.

[4]Alexander Campbell, "Letter from Australia," *MH* 5, no. 1 (January, 1862): 19.

[5]"An Address Delivered at the Annual Meeting of the Christian Missionary Society, A. D. 1857," *MH* 7, no. 11 (November, 1857): 607; see also "Church Edification," p. 542.

[6]"Practical Thoughts and Reflections," *MH* 3, no. 6 (June, 1846): 350.

[7]"Pre-eminence of Preaching in Public Worship," *MH* 6, no. 4 (April, 1862): 154

[8]"A Familiar Dialogue, Between the Editor and a Clergyman," Part I, *CB* 1, no. 12 (June 5, 1824): 233.

[9]Alexander Campbell, "Acts of the Apostles—Analysis of Section IV," *MH* 3, no. 6 (June, 1846): 350.

[10]"Dr. Chalmer's Experiment," *MH* 4, no. 5 (May, 1854): 272.

[11]"Missions and Missionaries," *MH* 4, no. 21 (December, 1861): 666-667.

[12]Robert Richardson writes at length on this Campbellian emphasis regarding the importance of righteous living as opposed to correct thinking on theological themes. See his "Nature of Christian Doctrine—No. II," *MH* 6, no. 4 (April, 1856): 205-211.

[13]Alexander Campbell, "Church Edification, *etc.*," *MH* 3, no. 10 (October, 1853): 544-546.

[14]"Use and Abuse of Preaching—No. III," *MH* 3, no. 6 (June, 1846): 318.

[15]Campbell says regarding the deacon that: "there is not a single intimation that preaching or teaching is any part of his office." "The Permanent Orders of the Ministry," *MH* 5, no. 11 (November, 1855): 626.

[16]"The Clergy—No. IV," *CB* 1, no. 6 (January 5, 1824): 109.

[17]"'The Origin' of the Christian Clergy, Splendid Meeting House, and Fixed Salaries, Exhibited from Ecclesiastical History," *CB* 1, no. 1 (July, 1823): 20.

[18]"Support of the Christian Ministry—No. II," *MH* 1, no. 11 (November, 1851): 638.

[19]"The Christian Ministry and Its Support—No. I," *MH* 7, no. 9 (September, 1850): 481.

[20]"The Duty and Means of Supporting Evangelists—No. I," *MH* 4, no. 4 (April, 1840): 180.

[21]"Quarterly Meeting," *CB* 5, no. 7 (February 5, 1828): 173.

[22]"Ancient Order of Things—No. XXX Official Names and Titles," *CB* 7, no. 2 (September 7, 1829): 48.

[23]In this lesser sense Campbell, for example, pleads "for many preachers like sister Bullard" who had led her children to Christ and had encouraged three of her four sons to become evangelists. "Sister Bullard," *MH* 6, no. 7 (July, 1849): 378.

[24]"Letters to England," *MH* 1, no. 7 (July, 1837): 317.

[25]*The Christian System,* fifth ed. (Cincinnati: Standard Publishing Co., 1901), p. 67.

[26]"Elder J. B. Ferguson's Relation of Pastor and People—No. I," *MH* 4, no. 10 (October, 1854): 566.

[27]Alexander Campbell, "Incidents on a Tour to the South—No. VI," *MH* 3, no. 6 (June, 1839), p. 265. See also "Evangelists and Pastors," *MH* 7, no. 1 (January, 1850): 23.

[28]"Synopsis of Reformation Principles and Objects," *MH* 1, no. 12 (December, 1837): 534.

[29]"An Excursion of Sixteen Hundred Miles," *MH* 3, no. 7 (July, 1853): 400. See also *The Christian System*, p. 61.

References

[30] "A Restoration of the Ancient Order of Things—No. XII. The Bishop's Office," *CB* 3, no. 9 (April 3, 1826): 187.

[31] "Miscellaneous Letters—No. I," *CB* 5, no. 2 (September 3, 1827): 73-74.

[32] *Memoirs*, II, p. 199.

[33] "'Hints' to the Advocates of a Restoration of the Ancient Order of Things and to the Proclaimers of the Ancient Gospel," *MH* 1, no. 8 (August 2, 1830): 366.

[34] "The Christian Preacher—No. VI," *MH* 3, no. 9 (September 3, 1832): 469. See also *MH* 5, no. 9 (September, 1834): 460.

[35] "Church Edification," *MH* 3, no. 10 (October, 1853): 542.

[36] "Organization—No. I," *MH* 5, no. 7 (July, 1855): 377.

[37] "A Restoration to An Ancient Order of Things: No. XIII. The Bishop's Office—No. II," *CB* 3, no. 11 (June 5, 1826): 216.

CHAPTER IV—Call and Character

[1] *Memoirs*, 1, p. 138.

[2] "Review of a Sermon," *CB* 3, no. 7 (March 6, 1826): 154-156. Campbell stood willing to deny in debate the proposition "That the Presbyterian clergy, or any other fraternity of Paido [sic]—Baptist clergy, is an order of men divinely constituted and authorized." See "Notification," *CB* 3, no. 1 (July 16, 1825): p. 16.

[3] "To Dr. A. Straith," *CB* 7, no. 5 (September 5, 1829): 108.

[4] "To Bishop R. B. Semple—Letter V," *CB* 5, no. 9 (April 7, 1828): 276.

[5] *Memoirs*, 2, pp. 332-333.

[6] "Letter to the Editor," *CB* 5, no. 7 (February 5, 1828): 169.

[7] "The Christian Religion The Clergy—No. I," *CB* 1, no. 3 (October 6, 1823): 54.

[8] "The Christian Religion The Clergy—No. I, *CB* 1, no. 3 (October 6, 1823). See also "Remarks on Missionaries," *CB* 1, no. 2 (September 1, 1823): 42.

[9] "A Years Labor," *CB* 5, no. 7 (February 5, 1828): 173.

[10] "Incidents on a Tour to Nashville, Tennessee—No. VI," *MH* 2, no. 3 (March 7, 1831): 114.

[11] "Colleges," *MH* 7, no. 5 (May, 1843): 213.

[12] "A Familiar Dialogue, Between the Editor and a Clergyman. Part II," *CB* 2, no. 1 (August 2, 1824): 19. See also "Remarks on Missionaries," *CB* 1, no. 2 (September 1, 1823): 42.

[13] "An Address," *MH* 3, no. 11 (November, 1853): 606.

[14] "A Familiar Dialogue, Between the Editor and a Clergyman. Part I," *CB* 1, no. 12 (June 5, 1824): 233.

[15] "Essays on the Work of the Holy Spirit in the Salvation of Men—No. IV," *CB* 2, no. 4 (November 1, 1824): 71. See also "Abuses of Christianity," *CB* 1, no. 4 (November 3, 1823): 77.

[16] "The Voice of God and the Word of God," *MH* 1, no. 3 (March 1, 1830): 126.

[17] *CB* 1, no. 11 (June 7, 1824): 217.

[18] "The Regeneration of the Church," *MH* 2, no. 6 (August 5, 1833): 375.

[19] "Incidents on a Tour to Nashville, Tennessee—No. VI," *MH* 2, no. 3 (March 7, 1831): 114.

[20] Alexander Campbell, "Sermons to Young Preachers—No. IV," *CB* 7, no. 9 (April 5, 1830): 214-216. Campbell constantly reiterated the parent's place as preacher to their children. See "Ancient Order of Things—No. XXX Official Names and Titles," *CB* 7, no. 2 (September 7, 1829): 47; "The Three Ages. Jewish Age—No. XIII," *CB* 7, no. 9 (April 5, 1830): 210; "Address to Christian Mothers," *CB* 1, no. 11 (June 7, 1824): 213.

[21] "To Epaphras—No. III," a letter signed by R. Richardson, S. Maxwell and A. Campbell, *MH* 3, no. 10 (October 1, 1832): 50.

[22] "Answers to S. B. Giles: 'Evangelists and pastors'," *MH* 7, no. 1 (January, 1850), 23.

[23] "Reply to Timothy," *MH* 5, no. 7 (July, 1834): 316. See *Memoirs*, 2, p. 130 and "Co-operation of Churches—No. III," *MH* 2, no. 6 (June 6, 1831): 243.

[24] *Memoirs*, 1, p. 148.

[25] *Memoirs*, 1, p. 381.

[26] Alexander Campbell, "The Clergy—No. IV," *CB* 1, no. 6 (January 5, 1824): 105-106.

[27] 6, no. 9 (September, 1849): 502-504.

[28] "Letters No, XXXI," *MH* 5, no. 9 (September, 1848): 521.

[29] "Letters from Europe—No. XX," *MH* 5, no. 1 (January, 1848): 30.

[30] "Bishops," *MH* 1, no. 9 (September 6, 1830): 428. On two occasions (October 22 and 29, 1810) Campbell advertised in *The Reporter* his sermon to be brought before the Christian Association of Washington and placed the initials V. D. S. after his name (*i.e., Verbi Divini Servus*, Servant of the Word of God). See *Memoirs*, I, p. 335.

[31] *Memoirs*, 2, p. 583. See also "Sermons to Young Preachers No. II," *CB* 7, no. 5 (December 5, 1829): 105.

[32] "'Campbellism' from the Watchman of the Prairies," *MH* 1, no. 2 (February, 1851): 83.

[33] *MH* 6, no. 6 (June, 1862): 250.

[34]"Extracts from My Sentimental Journal. No. III," *CB* 2, no. 12 (July 4, 1825): 248; "Remarks on Missionaries," *CB* 1, no. 2 (September 1, 1823): 38; "American Bible Society," *MH* 2, no. 2 (October 19, 1829): 76.

[35]"Tracts for Tennessee Baptists," *MH* 4, no. 9 (September, 1854): 497.

[36]Footnote by Alexander Campbell to a letter from S. G. Marshall, *CB* 5, no. 11 (June 2, 1828): 260.

[37]"Notes on a Tour to Illinois," *MH* 4, no. 3 (March, 1853): 139.

[38]"An Excursion to Kentucky and Henry Female College," *MH* 6, no. 7 (July, 1856): 395.

[39]Selina Huntington Campbell, *Home Life and Reminiscenses of Alexander Campbell* (St. Louis: John Burns, 1882), p. 253.

[40]*MH* 2, no. 1 (January, 1845): 13.

[41]*Memoirs*, 1, p. 138.

[42]"Introductory Remarks," *MH* 3, no. 1 (January 2, 1832): 3.

[43]"Ministerial Character—No. I," *MH* 2, no. 1 (January, 1845): 16.

[44]"Letters to My Co-Editors—No. II," *MH* 7, no. 4 (April, 1850): 223.

[45]"Reformation—No. IV, Reformation of the Preachers of Reformation," *MH* 6, no. 3 (March, 1835): 136.

[46]Alexander Campbell, "Preface," *MH* 1, no. 1 (January, 1851): 4.

[47]"Notes on a Tour to New York—No. 6," *MH* 5, no. 2 (February, 1834): 79.

[48]"To the Editor of the Christian Baptist," *CB* 4, no. 6 (January 1, 1827): 115; "Letter to Brother Campbell from R. B. S.," *CB* 3, no. 9 (April 3, 1826): 177.

[49]"Short Sermons for Business Men—No. IX," *MH* 4, no. 1 (January, 1861): 32.

CHAPTER V—Mankind and Mission

[1]In Antioch the Railway Depot while holding three thousand could not accommodate the crowds. See "An Excursion of Sixteen Hundred Miles," *MH* 3, no. 7 (July, 1853): 406.

[2]"Our Tour to the Far West—No. I," *MH* 3, no. 2 (February, 1846): 70; "Tour of Forty Days, etc. No. II," *MH* 1, no. 2 (February, 1851): 78.

[3]Alexander Campbell, "Ohio Meetings," *MH* 1, no. 10 (October, 1851): 599; "Letters to my Co-editors," *MH* 7, no. 4 (April, 1850): 219, 223.

4"Notes on a Tour to the South—No. I," *MH* 2, no. 6 (June, 1845): 244.

5"Letters from Europe—No. XII," *MH* 4, no. 11 (November, 1847): 618.

6*Mark Twain's Autobiography*, Vol. II, (Harper and Brothers Company, 1924) Reprinted by Clara Clemens Samossoud as quoted by Perry Epler Gresham, "Alexander Campbell—Schoolmaster," in *The Sage of Bethany—A Pioneer in Broadcloth* (St. Louis: The Bethany Press, 1960), p. 15.

7*Memoirs*, 1, pp. 469-470.

8Amos Sutton Hayden, *Early History of the Disciples in the Western Reserve, Ohio* (Cincinnati: Chase and Hall, 1875), p. 390.

9"European Tour," *MH* 4, no. 9 (September, 1847): 515.

10"A. Campbell's First Public Lecture in Edinburgh," *British Millennial Harbinger*, Vol. I (London: Simphin, Marshall and Co., 1848), p. 252.

11"An Excursion of Sixteen Hundred Miles," *MH* 3, no. 7 (July, 1853): 402; "Notes on a Tour, etc.—No. III," *MH* 2, no. 1 (January 3, 1831): 26.

12"Tour of Forty Days, *etc.* No. II," *MH* 3, no. 2 (February, 1851): 81.

13John Allen Gano, "News from the Churches," *MH* 3, no. 10 (October, 1839): 469. See also "Notes on a Tour to New York—No. III," *MH* 4, no. 12 (December, 1833): 598.

14"Letter from W. K. Pendleton," *MH* 1, no. 5 (May, 1858): 246.

15"Notes on a Tour to New York—No. V," *MH* 5, no. 1 (January, 1834): 38.

16"Notes on a Tour, *etc.*—No. III," *MH* 2, no. 1 (January 3, 1831): 24.

17"Notes on a Tour to the South—No. V," *MH* 3, no. 5 (May, 1839): 201.

18"Notes on a Tour to the South—No. I," *MH* 7, no. 6 (June, 1857): 313.

19"Notes on a Tour in Illinois," *MH* 7, no. 12 (December, 1857): 706.

20Alexander Campbell, "Notes on a Tour to Illinois—No. III," *MH* 4, no. 1 (January, 1854): 48; H. Hussey, "A Visit to Elder A. Campbell at Bethany," *MH* 4, no. 11 (November, 1854): 648.

21Selina Huntington Campbell, *Home Life and Reminiscences*, p. 448; W. K. Pendleton, "Notes on a Tour for Bethany College," *MH* 1, no. 3 (March, 1858): 157. See also *Memoirs* 2, p. 91.

22"In Memoriam," *MH* 37, no. 7 (July, 1866): 317.

References

23"The Christian Preacher—No. I," *MH* 3, no. 1 (January 2, 1832): 27.

24"The Religion of Excitement, and the Excitement of Religion," *MH* 3, no. 1 (January, 1839): 34.

25"The Christian Preacher—No. IV," *MH* 3, no. 7 (July 2, 1832): 310.

26"Sermons to Young Preachers—No. III," *CB* 7, no. 8 (March 1, 1830): 184.

27Alexander Campbell, ed., *Debate on the Evidences of Christianity* (Bethany, Va.: Alexander Campbell, 1829), p. 463.

28"Response to Dr. Humphrey's Letters—No. IV," *MH* 7, no. 8 (August, 1850): 434.

29An Observer, "Methodistic Enthusiasm—No. II," *MH* 2, no. 1 (January, 1845): 11. Cf. "Modern Proselytism—No. II," *MH* 5, no. 7 (July, 1841): 306.

30"Incidents on a Tour to the S.—No. I," *MH* 3, no. 1 (January, 1839), p. 12.

31Isaac Errett, editor of the Christian Standard, quoted by Archibald McLean, *Alexander Campbell, as a Preacher* (Grand Rapids: Fleming H. Revell Company, 1908), p. 17.

32*Memoirs*, 2, p. 514.

33"Dr. Heman Humphrey's Letters—No. I," *MH* 7, no. 5 (May, 1850): 273-274.

34"The Patriarchal Age—No. VI," *CB* 6, no. 6 (January 5, 1829): 140; cf. 141.

35"Notes on a Tour to New York—No. VI," *MH* 5, no. 2 (February, 1834): 78.

36"Doctrine Not Faith—No. I," *MH* 2, no. 11 (November, 1859): 641; cf. "Is Christianity a System?" *MH* 5, no. 2 (February, 1862): 77.

37"Letters from the Senior Editor," *MH* 2, no. 7 (July, 1859): 380.

38*The Christian System*, p. 94. Campbell reprinted in the *Christian Baptist* St. Anthony of Padua, Italy's "A Sermon to Fish," commenting that modern sermons often addressed men as if they were but fish and incapable of being moved by testimony. See Vol. I, no. 5 (December 1, 1823): 96.

39"Faith, Hope, Love," *MH* 1, no. 5 (May, 1858): 382.

40Quotation from Campbell's sermon on Romans 10:4 (April 7, 1811) in *Memoirs*, 1, p. 376.

41"An Excursion of Sixteen Hundred Miles," *MH* 3, no. 7 (July, 1853): 405.

[42]"Extracts from My Sentimental Journal," *CB* 1, no. 9 (April 5, 1824): 173.

[43]"Reply," *CB* 2, no. 9 (April 4, 1825): 179.

[44]"Tracts for the People—No. XXXIV," *MH* 6, no. 7 (July, 1849): 370.

[45]"The Voice of God and the Word of God," *MH* 1, no. 3 (March, 1830): 126.

[46]"Converting Power," *MH* 4, no. 10 (October, 1833): 496.

[47]"To Mr. William Jones, of London. Letter III," *MH* 6, no. 2 (February, 1835): 81.

CHAPTER VI—Matter and Manner

[1]"Address to the Readers of the Christian Baptist," *CB* 5, no. 9 (April 7, 1828): 262.

[2]"Replication No. II To Spencer Clack," *CB* 5, no. 2 (September 3, 1827): 42.

[3]Alexander Campbell, "Reply to a Universal Discussion," *MH* 3, no. 1 (January, 1839): 33.

[4]"Orthodoxy—No. II," *MH* 7, no. 2 (February, 1857): 76.

[5]"Letters to England," *MH* 1, no. 7 (July, 1837): 317-318.

[6]"Means of Regeneration—No. II, Response," *MH* 6, no. 2 (February, 1856): 69.

[7]"Tracts for Ireland—No. II," *MH* 3, no. 9 (September, 1853): 500.

[8]"Letter to William Jones," *MH* 5, no. 11 (December, 1834): 586.

[9]*Ibid.*, p. 587.

[10]SILAS, "The Crisis—No. IV," *MH* 1, no. 6 (June, 1844): 272.

[11]"Letters from Europe—No. XXVII," *MH* 5, no. 5 (May, 1848): 272. When Mr. Robertson asked Campbell to speak on slavery in Edinburgh, he replied, "The Gospel, and Church, and not Slavery nor Abolition, were the objects of his mission." See Selina Huntington Campbell, *Home Life and Reminiscenses*, pp. 379-380.

[12]Daniel Webster, "Choice Selections," *MH* 3, no. 12 (December, 1853): 701.

[13]"Incidents on a Tour to the South—No. II," *MH* 3, no. 2 (February, 1839): 55.

[14]"Political Reverends," *MH* 6, no. 12 (December, 1835): 594.

[15]"Dr. Chalmer's Experiment," *MH* 4, no. 5 (May, 1854): 272. See also Wayland and Campbell, "The Christian Ministry," *MH* 4, no. 6 (June, 1854): 312.

References

[16] "Sermon on the Law," *MH* 3, no. 9 (September, 1846): 513.

[17] *Ibid.*, p. 513.

[18] "'Address' to the Readers of the Christian Baptist—No. II," *CB* 1, no. 6 (January 5, 1824): 116.

[19] "Church Edification," *MH* 3, no. 10 (October, 1853): 543.

[20] "Peter's Second Speech," *MH* 3, no. 4 (April, 1846): 231.

[21] Alexander Campbell, "Peter's Second Speech," *MH* 3, no. 4 (April, 1846): 231.

[22] "Dr. Chalmer's Experiment," *MH* 4, no. 5 (May, 1854): 273; cf. *Memoirs* 2, p. 655.

[23] (Centreville, Kentucky: Published for R. B. Neal, 1891).

[24] Thomas W. Grafton, *Alexander Campbell Leader of the Great Reformation of the Nineteenth Century* (St. Louis: Christian Publishing Company, 1897), p. 180.

[25] *Memoirs*, 2, p. 93.

[26] "Extracts from My Sentimental Journal. No. III," *CB* 2, no. 12 (July 4, 1825): 248.

[27] J. A. Williams, *Life of Elder John Smith*, p. 133.

[28] "Practical Thoughts and Reflections," *MH* 4, no. 3 (March, 1847): 154.

[29] "Practical Thoughts and Reflections," *MH* 4, no. 3 (March, 1847): 154.

[30] "A Good Library," *MH* 5, no. 10 (October, 1834): 490.

[31] "Sermons to Young Preachers," *CB* 7, no. 2 (September 7, 1829): 46.

[32] "Use and Abuse of Preaching," *MH* 3, no. 5 (May, 1846): 25.

[33] "The Anglo-Saxon Languages," *Popular Lectures and Addresses* (Philadelphia: James Challen and Son, 1861), p. 19.

[34] Vol. I, no. 10 (May 3, 1824): 201.

[35] "Letters from Europe," *MH* 4, no. 10 (October, 1847): 551.

[36] W. T. Moore, ed., *Familiar Lectures*, p. iii.

[37] Alexander Campbell, "A. Campbell's Orations. A letter to Brother Wallis," *The Christian Messenger and Family Magazine*, 3 (1847): 375.

CHAPTER VII—Molds and Models

[1] "On Teaching Christianity—No. III," *CB* 1, no. 6 (January 5, 1824): 113.

[2] Alexander Campbell, "Texts and Textuary Divines," *CB* 2, no. 10 (May 2, 1825): 189. In this article, Campbell recalls hearing at age fourteen a sermon by a Scotch preacher on "Malt." The

acrostic called for a *M*etaphorical, *A*llegorical, *L*iteral and *T*heological interpretation of texts and also dealt with *M*urder, *A*dultery, *L*asciviousness and *T*reason with their resulting *M*isery, *A*nguish, *L*amentation and *T*orment.

³*Memoirs*, I, pp. 131-132.

⁴*A Memorial Discourse on the Occasion of the Death of President Alexander Campbell* (Baltimore: Innes and Maguire, 1866), p. 13.

⁵"To the Disciples of Christ Residing in Kansas," *MH* 7, no. 8 (September, 1857): 524.

⁶"The Editor's Reply to Brother Garnett," *MH* 7, no. 6 (June, 1836): 245.

⁷In his *Popular Lectures and Addresses* (Philadelphia: James Challen and Son, 1863), are preserved thirty-seven addresses on as many themes.

⁸"The Verse-A-Day System, *etc.*" *Ibid.*, p. 313. A portion of this education was in Ahorey. Three years were in his uncles' (Archibald and Enos) academy near Newry.

CHAPTER VIII—Life and Labors

¹*Memoirs*, I, pp. 101-102.

²This sermon may be found complete in *MH* 3, no. 9 (September, 1846) and in Selina Huntington Campbell, *Home Life, etc.*, pp. 191-236, and in part in Richardson, *Memoirs*, 1, pp. 469-479.

³Quoted in Selina Campbell, *Home Life*, p. 192.

⁴Manuscript No. 332 of the material found in Australia contains a sermon on the same text, Romans 8:3, delivered June 6, 1813 at Cadiz and a similar message on Romans 6:14, delivered October 23, 1812 at Brush Run.

⁵Such as "Is Moral Philosophy an Inductive Science?" given June 16, 1840 before the Jeffersonian Society of the University of Virginia; "Demonology" delivered March 10, 1841 before the Popular Lecture Club of Nashville, Tennessee; "Primary or Common Schools" delivered September 8, 1841 in Clarksburg, Virginia; "Responsibility of Men of Genius" delivered August 6, 1844 before the Union Literary Society of Miami University, Ohio; "The Anglo-Saxon Language—Its Origin, Character and Destiny" delivered December 11, 1849 before the Young Men's Mercantile Library Association; "The Destiny of Our Country" delivered August 3, 1852 before the Philo-Literary Society of Jefferson College; "Phrenology, Animal Magnetism; Spirit Rappings, *etc.*" de-

References

livered September 28, 1852 before the Washington Literary Society of Washington College; "The True Basis of all Moral Science" delivered April 13, 1856 before the Athenium.

⁶"Notes of Incidents on a Tour Through Illinois and Missouri—No. III," *MH* 3, no. 3 (March, 1853): 127-128.

⁷Selina Huntington Campbell, *Home Life*, p. 253.

CHAPTER IX—Sources and Structure

¹*Psalms, Hymns, and Spiritual Songs, Adapted to the Christian Religion, Selected by Alexander Campbell*, 2d ed., (Bethany, Brooke County, Virginia: Printed and Published by A. Campbell, 1829).

²Campbell preached a communion sermon from Song of Solomon 2:8-13 on May 5, 1811 at Brush Run, calling the language of the text "human and natural" but the ideas "spiritual and supernatural" (Manuscript D).

³"An Address," *MH* 2, no. 4 (April, 1852): 181 ff. This was also his topic when such a text as Malachi 3 was used in 1826 at the meeting of the Mahoning Baptist Association. See "Anecdotes, Incidents, and Facts," *MH* 6, no. 1 (January, 1849): 46.

⁴Campbell preached December 2, 1812 from Exodus 19-20 and Hebrews 9:9 on the typology of the court, walls and holy place of the Tabernacle (Manuscript No. 332) and at another time Exodus 25:27-28 on the furniture (Manuscript No. 332).

⁵"Leaves from a Life," quoted from *CB*, in the *Christian Standard* (October 15, 1898), p. 1.

⁶Nicholas Jackson, "Notices," in *Bible Advocate* (England) quoted in "European Tour," *MH* 4, no. 9 (September, 1847): 515.

⁷Selina Campbell, *Home Life*, p. 356.

⁸"Letters from Europe," *MH* 5, no. 10 (October, 1848): 573.

⁹Microfilm prepared in Australia, on file at the Disciples of Christ Historical Society labeled "News Clippings, *etc.*"

¹⁰"Notes on a Tour to Eastern Virginia—No. II," *MH* 6, no. 3 (March, 1856): 137.

¹¹"Humble Beginnings," *MH* 6, no. 1 (January, 1842): 5.

¹²*Memoirs*, 2, pp. 336-337.

¹³Manuscript D.

¹⁴"An Address on Education," *MH* 6, no. 11 (November, 1856): 635.

¹⁵Sermon on Matthew 16:26 in Manuscript E.

¹⁶"Notes on a Tour—No. III," *MH* 2, no. 1 (January, 1831): 28.

[17]Manuscript No. 332.

[18]"Notes on a Tour to Illinois—No. III," *MH* 4, no. 1 (January, 1854): 44.

[19]"Incidents on a Tour to Nashville, Tennessee—No. VI," *MH* 2, no. 3 (March, 1831): 116; cf. *Memoirs*, 2, p. 635.

[20]Sermon on John 18:36 in Manuscript D.

[21]Sermon on Revelation 20:11-13 in Manuscript E.

[22]Sermon on Titus 1:5 in Manuscript F.

[23]Sermon on Matthew 11:25-27 in Manuscript F.

[24]Alexander Campbell, "Notes on a Tour to the South—No. II," *MH* 7, no. 8 (September, 1857): 506.

[25]"Incidents on a Tour to Nashville—No. V," *MH* 2, no. 2 (February, 1831): 54-60.

[26]Manuscript F.

[27]Alexander Campbell, "Notes on a Tour to New York—No. V," *MH* 5, no. 1 (January, 1834): 37.

[28]Alexander Campbell, "Short Sermons on Christian Practice," *MH* 3, no. 5 (May, 1839): 204.

[29]Manuscript D.

[30]"An Address," *MH* 3, no. 11 (November, 1853): 606.

[31]*Memoirs*, 2, p. 594.

[32]Manuscript F.

[33]Quoted in Archibald McLean, *Alexander Campbell as a Preacher*, reprint of 1908 ed. by Fleming H. Revell Company, (Grand Rapids, Michigan: Baker Book House, 1955), p. 11.

[34]Mrs. Eliza Davies, *The Story of an Earnest Life: A Woman's Adventure in Australia, and in Two Voyages Around the World* (Cincinnati: Central Book Concern, 1881), pp. 239-240.

[35]"Model of a Discourse, No. II," *MH* 3, no. 8 (August, 1832): 400.

[36]"Letters to England—No. VIII," *MH* 2, no. 4 (April, 1838): 181.

[37]Archibald McLean, *Thomas and Alexander Campbell* (Cincinnati: Foreign Christian Missionary Society, 1930), p. 51.

[38]*Memoirs*, 2, p. 585.

[39]"Practical Thoughts and Reflections," *MH* 5, no. 3 (March, 1848): 140.

[40]"Sermons to Young Preachers—No. IV," *CB* 7, no. 9 (April 5, 1830): 213.

[41]"Publications," *MH* 1, no. 5 (May, 1837): 237.

[42]Alexander Campbell, *Popular Lectures and Addresses* (Philadelphia: James Challen & Son, 1864), p. 68.

References

43*MH* 1, no. 3 (March, 1830): 138.

44Quoted in Archibald McLean, *Alexander Campbell as a Preacher*, p. 11.

45"Elder J. B. Ferguson's Relation of Pastor and People, No. I," *MH* 4, no. 10 (October, 1854): 564.

CHAPTER X—Impact and Impression

1Quoted by Alexander Campbell in "Little Things," *CB* 2, no. 7 (February 7, 1825): 144.

2Quoted in *MH* 1, no. 2 (February, 1851): 82-83.

3Quoted in *CB* 7, no. 9 (April 5, 1830): 233.

4John Augustus Williams, *Life of Elder John Smith with some account of the Rise and Progress of the current Reformation* (Cincinnati: Standard Publishing Company, 1904), p. 121.

5"Correspondence," *Christian Standard* (August 15, 1868).

6(St. Louis: Christian Publishing Company, 1897).

7Quoted in "European Tour," *MH* 4, no. 9 (September, 1847): 515.

8*Memoirs*, 2, p. 164.

9Benjamin Lyon Smith, *Alexander Campbell* (St. Louis: The Bethany Press, 1930), p. 262.

10Amos Sutton Hayden, *Early History of the Disciples in the Western Reserve, Ohio* (Cincinnati: Chase and Hall, 1875), p. 391.

11Samuel Rogers quoted in Richardson, *Memoirs*, 2, p. 333.

12Eliza Davies, *The Story of an Earnest Life: A Woman's Adventures in Australia, and in Two Voyages Around the World* (Cincinnati: Central Book Concern, 1881), p. 240.

13Entry for October 28, 1858 in Unpublished diary among the MSS at the College of the Bible, Lexington, Kentucky.

14Williams, *Life of Elder John Smith*, p. 132.

15Archibald McLean, *Alexander Campbell as a Preacher* (Grand Rapids: Fleming H. Revell Company, 1908), p. 12.

16Quoted from the *New York Observer* by William Baxter, "Alexander Campbell and Walter Scott as Preachers," *The British Harbinger* (September 1, 1869), p. 290.

17Quoted in *Autobiography of Benjamin Johnson Radford* (Eureka, Illinois: n.p., 1928), p. 14.

18Entry of August 6, 1844 in an unpublished "Journal kept at Miami University 1843-1848" quoted by Albert A. Gonse, Jr., "A Rhetorical Analysis and Criticism of Selected Occasional Addresses of Alexander Campbell 1838-1858, Unpublished M. A. thesis (University of Alabama, 1950), p. 58. Cp. W. C. Rogers,

Recollections of Men of Faith (St. Louis: Christian Publishing Company, 1889), pp. 13-16.

[19]Such as George D. Prentice of the *Louisville Journal.*

[20]Such as Frances Trollope, *Domestic Manners of Americans* (New York: Dodd, Meade and Company, 1832) I, p. 149 ff.

[21]Such as Theodore S. Ball of Louisville.

[22]Such as Chief Justice Jeremiah Sullivan Black of Pennsylvania (later Attorney-General of the United States.)

[23]Such as General Robert E. Lee.

[24]Such as President Madison and President Buchanan.

[25]Such as Thomas Armitage, *A History of the Baptists* (New York: Bryan, Baylor, and Company, 1887), p. 736.

[26]Such as the *Protestant Churchman* quoted in Richardson, *Memoirs*, 2, p. 513.

[27]Such as the *National Christian Advocate* quoted in *MH* 5, no. 1 (January, 1855): 42-45 or Bishop Warren A. Changler, *The South in the Building of the Nation*, 10, p. 525.

[28]Such as the *Protestant Herald*, quoted in *MH* 1, no. 4 (April, 1844): 181-182.

[29]Such as Archbishop Purcell quoted in John Allen Hudson, *The Man and the Moment* (Cincinnati: Christian Leader Corporation, 1927), p. 117.

[30]Such as the Society of Moral Philanthropists quoted in *MH* 5, no. 2 (February, 1834): 80.

[31]Alexander Campbell, "The School of Preachers," *MH* 6, no. 10 (October, 1835): 478-479; see also *MH* 7, no. 1 (January, 1836): 45-46 and 3, no. 10 (October, 1839): 466-467.

[32]Later these became annual for practical reasons. See "Anecdotes, Incidents, and Facts," *MH* 5, no. 9 (September, 1848): 524.

[33]"Anecdotes," *MH* 7, no. 6 (June, 1836): 245.

[34]"Welshimer and Ames: A Comparison," Vol. 82, no. 46 (November 15, 1944): 1101.

[35]Granville T. Walker, *Preaching in the Thought of Alexander Campbell* (St. Louis: The Bethany Press, 1954), p. 121.

[36]Stephen J. England, "Alexander Campbell's Views on Baptism in the Light of the Ecumenical Movement," in Perry Epler Gresham, *The Sage of Bethany: A Pioneer in Broadcloth* (St. Louis: The Bethany Press, 1960), pp. 108-109.

[37]Alexander Campbell, "Faith, Hope, Love," *MH* 1, no. 5 (May, 1858): 282.